PUBLIC SPEAKING

How to Develop Self-confidence and Influence
People by Effective Social Skills

(Public Speaking and Presentation Skills to Make
Your Presence Felt and Speak Without Fear)

Dale Nihill

Published by Rob Miles

© **Dale Nihill**

All Rights Reserved

Public Speaking: How to Develop Self-confidence and Influence People by Effective Social Skills (Public Speaking and Presentation Skills to Make Your Presence Felt and Speak Without Fear)

ISBN 978-1-7771171-9-1

All rights reserved. No part of this guide may be reproduced in any form without permission in writing from the publisher except in the case of brief quotations embodied in critical articles or reviews.

Legal & Disclaimer

The information contained in this book is not designed to replace or take the place of any form of medicine or professional medical advice. The information in this book has been provided for educational and entertainment purposes only.

The information contained in this book has been compiled from sources deemed reliable, and it is accurate to the best of the Author's knowledge; however, the Author cannot guarantee its accuracy and validity and cannot be held liable for any errors or omissions. Changes are periodically made to this book. You must consult your doctor or get professional medical advice before using any of the suggested remedies, techniques, or information in this book.

Upon using the information contained in this book, you agree to hold harmless the Author from and against any damages, costs, and expenses, including any legal fees potentially resulting from the application of any of the information provided by this guide. This disclaimer applies to any damages or injury caused by the use and application, whether directly or indirectly, of any advice or information presented, whether for breach of contract, tort, negligence, personal injury, criminal intent, or under any other cause of action.

You agree to accept all risks of using the information presented inside this book. You need to consult a professional medical practitioner in order to ensure you are both able and healthy enough to participate in this program.

Table of Contents

INTRODUCTION 1

CHAPTER 1: SUPER SPEECH AND ITS POWERS 6

CHAPTER 2: BODY LANGUAGE 14

CHAPTER 3: BREATHING EXERCISES 19

CHAPTER 4: BASICS ELEMENT OF COMMUNICATIONS 27

CHAPTER 5: HOW TO COMMUNICATE WITH PEOPLE TO BUILD FRIENDSHIPS 33

CHAPTER 6: GO PUBLIC 37

CHAPTER 7: YOUR IMAGE 42

CHAPTER 8: WHAT'S YOUR STORY? 50

CHAPTER 9: SPEAKING 101 58

CHAPTER 10: BASIC SIMPLE SPEECH STRUCTURE 63

CHAPTER 11: YOUR AUDIENCE'S HIDDEN SECRET, REVEALED 73

CHAPTER 12: FOCUS YOUR SPEECH ON THE AUDIENCE EXPECTATIONS 77

CHAPTER 13: MAKE OUT AN OUTLINE 82

CHAPTER 14: HOW TO GET RID OF THE FEAR OF PUBLIC SPEAKING USING THESE PROVEN TECHNIQUES 86

CHAPTER 15: HOW TO WRITE EFFECTIVE AND ENGAGING SPEECHES 96

CHAPTER 16: STORYTELLING 112

CHAPTER 17: HOW TO WRITE YOUR FIRST PUBLIC SPEAKING PRESENTATION... 115

CHAPTER 18: WHAT IS SPECIAL ABOUT THIS BOOK: AN INDISPENSABLE INTRODUCTION 123

CHAPTER 19: WHAT CAN YOU DO TO IMPROVE YOUR PUBLIC SPEAKING SKILLS... 128

CHAPTER 20: WHAT DOES BREAKING THE ICE ACTUALLY MEAN?... 139

CHAPTER 21: TIME MANAGEMENT AND GOAL SETTING 142

CHAPTER 22: FEAR IS INVISIBLE..................................... 155

CHAPTER 23: SHORT AND LONG SPEECHES 158

CHAPTER 24: DELIVERING YOUR SPEECH....................... 167

CONCLUSION.. 179

Introduction

In rhetoric, as in any science, there is basic knowledge - this is the theory, the basis of oratory.

Public speaking leads to wealth. They help build a network of acquaintances, relationships and increase the awareness of the audience about you. This can help to open up new directions in business, job offers, and, in general, increase your presence in social media.

Most people are not comfortable speaking to a large group of people. Entrepreneur.com has published research from the National Institute of Mental Health, which claims that 74% of adults suffer from a fear of public speaking. And you are definitely, most likely, one of those people. Get very nervous literally every time you go out on a big stage or face a camera? Well, you should know that most people feel the same way.

Using a proactive approach to develop your oratory and presentation skills can quickly build self-confidence. As your confidence grows, your excitement will gradually go away, regardless of the size of the hall where you have to speak.

This book describes how to make your speech vivid, inspiring, and memorable. The value of the book is also in its practical orientation. It gives a lot of advice on various aspects of oratory.

Let me quickly draw attention to the fact that in different chapters, different tenses are used. This is a technique that allows you to make the material more readable, a kind of change of tempo - rhythm. And accordingly, the reception of effects on consciousness. For example, using words such as "us," "we," I expect that thanks to this, the algorithm for working on public speaking will be remembered quickly, easily, and forever. And in the different parts of the book, where various tips and observations of mine are given, an appeal to "you" follows. This means that you (the reader) yourself decide to take advantage of these tips and tricks, or to develop your own oratory and style.

There are several exercises for independent work, by which you will develop the skill of composing the text of a public speech, as well as directly - conducting the speech itself.

First, you should know - "Every speech should be like a living being - it should have a body with its head and legs, and the trunk and limbs should fit together and fit the whole" - Plato. So, we are confronted with the fact of the need to speak publicly. We have to speak at the anniversary of an enterprise, presentation of the company, meeting of the board of directors of the corporation, gala, or just at a friendly party. "Where to start?"

This question excites everyone who is going to speak. What text to write to say what you need and make a good impression on the audience? And even deserve their applause? How to achieve your goal through public speaking? The answers to these questions are in this book, which presents my method of creating text, many times tested in practice.

First, do not panic, but tune in to work. Television journalists know that there is no topic that cannot be stated in 40 seconds. If they learned this, then everyone will learn. Secondly, to understand that all now self-confident, successful speakers, once also asked themselves the question: "Where to start?"

You need to start from scratch. Even if we are used to typing on a computer, you still need to start with a blank sheet of plain white paper. Until you learn to compose texts of public speeches quickly, which is called "on autopilot," you need to do a thorough preliminary study on the algorithms in this book. Desirable - by hand. And only after the elaboration is done, type the text on the computer. Why is that? When typing on a computer, only one fragment is visible, and when starting work, you need to see everything, and that's all: the topic, idea, task, composition, amount of content, etc. are best kept in front of your eyes by putting them written on the right side of the table, next to the computer. If writing by hand is not comfortable, you need to type, print, and put in front of your eyes. This will help to stay in line with the theme, tasks, and structure the material in accordance with the composition.

Ready?

Chapter 1: Super Speech and its Powers

Ever wondered how Adolf Hitler, Martin Luther King, and Ellen DeGeneres managed to have such huge followings? Let's skip the controversial talk about Hitler and King but focus on how DeGeneres' show is watched by millions every time it airs. Her show is entertaining but you get to have fun because she speaks. Every time she lets out words, you're just sucked into an hour of informative and amusing programming. That is the power of speech. And you can say that DeGeneres has developed such an ease with public speaking that it translates to a world-renowned quality in her presentations.

You may feel like you could never, in a million years, do what she can. You can't speak in front of people with such style and comfort. You can never imagine yourself not wetting your pants with fright with hundreds of eyes focusing on only you. As a kid, it's not that hard to speak your mind because we hardly have any concept of communication apprehension at age 5. We just talk and talk to anyone who listens. But I remember the first time I had to talk to a lot of people in grade school and all I wanted was to feign sickness and go home to cuddle with my mom. Most of us want to escape whenever the opportunity to speak publicly arises.

You may not be continuously and entirely aware of it but you actually engage in some form of public speech every day. You answer questions in class, deliver reports on certain topics, present an idea to two or three bosses, pitch in a suggestion during group discussion, etc. This goes to show that your skills at public speaking aren't completely nil. Now you just have to hone that skill in order to reap the benefits. The advantages it can provide you transcend the good grade that you'll get in class if you manage to deliver your presentation well, or the pat in the back from your boss if you presented your business proposal with success.

Speaking—publically or otherwise—is a pervasive activity and it's not something you can avoid because human interactions are better founded by the existence and maintenance of communication. The results of speaking effectively are likewise wide-reaching.

Effectively delivering a public speech and learning the skills required to do so will give you a great advantage in whatever field you are in. Generally, public speaking helps you become a more participative member of your community. It can help you advance your career and further your achievements. Learning how to speak with confidence is an additional skill that you can add to your repertoire of capabilities. Companies see it as a bonus if their prospective employees know how to effectively speak in public.

As public speaking skills are highly valued in today's business and academic status quo, one's reputation is enhanced if he possesses it. He will be viewed as an adept individual who one can call on whenever the need to present comes into the fore. Through the positive evaluations of colleagues and employers, among others, a public speaker's self-confidence receives a huge boost and will also set himself apart from competitors.

Case in point: two candidates vying for the same position, possessing more or less the same educational background, have to battle it out with skills at which they can proudly say they're proficient. If you're the employer, who would you pick: Candidate A whose communication skills need significant improvement or Candidate B who you can send right through the fire since he can talk his way through the flames?

For a businessperson, speaking adeptly would give you major advantage over other businesses. Since you can speak well, you can market your products well and advertise them to more people.

Attracting the right customers to your business is easily done if you know how to approach them verbally.

Because you can now speak despite any debilitating anxiety, you can meet new people, interact more effectively with them, and establish connections. Through your messages and the things you speak about, you can influence people into your way of thinking.

Public speaking can be categorized according to the purpose it would serve. Some people give speeches in order to inform and spread awareness to their audience. They want to help their listeners achieve knowledge that they don't possess yet so that this newly-acquired information can be understood and used to perform certain tasks.

The main goal of informative speeches is just to gain knowledge, not to push people into a specific way of using that knowledge because, by then, it would be the realm of persuasive speeches.

Other people deliver speeches to persuade others into their way of thinking, to encourage people to embrace a certain point of view, or practice a behavior that they haven't tried before. Presidential speeches during elections are the most common form of persuasion speeches as they aim to entice voters to accept the candidate and vote for him or her. The most distinguishing aspect of persuasive speech is how it calls for action or for a change in behavior and thinking among the audience.

It doesn't escape our notice when persuasive speeches are used to manipulate people. An advocate may attend a speaking engagement to talk about why we should donate to a certain charity and persuade the members of the audience to give a significant amount of their money to a certain bank account with funds for building a school. At face value, the speech is philanthropic and the message is something that should be supported wholeheartedly. If, however, the advocate is actually a scammer, he exhibits the power of speech and how it can be used to take advantage of other people.

The measure of success of a persuasive speech is the extent to which it has influenced people to enact its message. A speech about giving donations could measure its effectiveness by determining the amount donated to the intended institution.

Another purpose for public speaking is to entertain people. It differs from both informative and persuasive speeches, which stress the end result of the speech, because of how it puts more emphasis on the theme of the speech. This kind of speech is obviously very worthwhile to hear. They are packaged in different forms and can be humorous or serious. The primary function is to provide the audience an escape from their day-to-day lives and problems. Some examples of entertaining speeches include after-dinner speeches and inspirational speeches.

Chapter 2: Body Language

We are more than just verbal creatures. While we communicate with words, we also communicate with gestures — sometimes in ways that say more than mere words can. A person who tells you that they're in charge, but looks down and hunches while they do so, has less credibility than someone who stands up straight with feet apart and meets your gaze unflinchingly.

The latter doesn't even have to say a word. Their very stance speaks louder than the wimp who can't even look you straight in the eye.

So don't be a wimp.

I strongly advise you to practice your speech before a camera. Most computers today have a camera function which should allow you to see how well (or not) you come across. If you can't come across as convincing and confident when you're all alone before your camera, trust me when I say you'll come across worse before an audience.

When you do finally get up before an audience, try to be still, don't move, don't pace, and keep your hands at your sides, but not in your pockets. Meet some of their gazes briefly as you observe a moment of silence (how long depends on the gravity of your content), and be sure to have a slight smile.

This silent pause is a universal – and very powerful – signal to your audience that you have something to say, which will force them to be quiet so they can hear it. Your smile tells them you're a **decent** person with something to say and that they've nothing to fear from you. With the exception of a school lecture, most audience members attend a speech voluntarily, so scaring them off is **not** a good idea.

Just as a non-credible person can turn an audience off, so a hostile-seeming speaker can do the same.

On the topic of body languages, I've noticed that different cultures expect different things from a speaker. While not comprehensive, here are some general rules of thumb to consider:

☐ **American and Canadian audiences** seem to like confident and exuberant speakers, especially those who come across as the person-next-door type. It doesn't matter if it's Bill Gates speaking or some small town insurance salesman — the friendlier and more frank the speaker is, the more American and Canadian audiences seem to open up to them.

☐ **British audiences** pride themselves on being polite, but up to a point. There is an ancient tradition in England of heckling speakers if they bring up an unpleasant topic, as well as a tradition of said speakers stopping their speeches to address hecklers.

That aside, while exuberance in someone who is clearly excited about their topic is appreciated, over-exuberance is frowned upon. In Britain, I've attended many speeches given by overly-friendly and overly-excited Americans with genuinely interesting topics, only to feel embarrassed for the speaker because the audience has closed them off.

☐ **German and French audiences** prefer things straight and to the point. They tend to be as interested in credentials as they are in the subject matter, and most prefer hearing speeches that follow a news bulletin format. This means they prefer hearing the most relevant information first, and the least relevant last.

☐ **Chinese and Japanese audiences** tend to become guarded and retreat behind a mask when they are confronted by exuberant speakers. No matter how impressive a speaker's resume is, they have a preference for those who are humble and make use of few gestures.

Due to the similarity of their traditional educational systems, many have also developed the habit of **only** reacting to information **after** it has been presented. If you're expecting applause during parts of your speech, for example, you'll likely be disappointed. They consider it polite to wait until **after** the speech is over.

☐ **Overall**, you **have** to be aware of your audience and pay attention to how they react to **you**. Starting your speech by being still, keeping your hands at your sides, and observing a few moments of silence, seems to have the universal effect of getting everyone else to pay close attention. The trick from here on out is keeping them that way till the end of your speech.

Chapter 3: Breathing Exercises

When it comes to enhancing your speaking voice, you have to carry out a few breathing exercises in order to make it easier for you to speak efficiently. These exercises are directed towards your abdominal muscles in order to improve your voice. The key is to pay attention to the breathing, and listening to the air moving in and out of your lungs. You can carry out these exercises once a day for at least two weeks to see any improvement in your voice.

Here are some of the exercises to carry out:

Exercise one

Lie down on your back and place a book over your stomach or just your hands.

Draw in a deep breath through your mouth and feel the book or your hands rising up.

Release the breath through your mouth and feel the book moving down.

You have to be able to breathe in and out without much effort.

Exercise two

Sit on a chair and place your feet firmly on the ground.

Push your shoulders backwards and sit straight.

Place a hand over your stomach and breathe in from your nose and out from your mouth.

You have to feel your stomach moving in and out.

Your upper body must remain steady and you can consider sitting in front of a mirror while taking up this exercise.

Draw the breath in from your nose and release it from your mouth.

While doing so, begin humming by reciting "hummm."

The vibrations should move all throughout your body and especially around your nose area.

The sound should originate from your nose and not your lungs.

Now, release the air through your mouth and utter "up" or "hup."

Exercise three

Sit on a chair with your shoulders pulled back.

Draw in breaths from your mouth while saying "up one, up two, up three" until "up ten."

You have to draw in a breath after each phrase.

Once you start getting comfortable with it, you have to repeat the words faster.

An alternative to this method is to sit with a straight back and your shoulders pushed back.

Breathe in and out through your nose and say "run a mile" "get a paper" or "buy some food."

Release the breath from your mouth.

Exercise four

Sit on the chair with your shoulders pushed backwards.

Breathe in and out from your mouth while reading a book out loud.

Hold your breath for 10 syllables and then breathe out and so on.

Apart from these, there are some basic exercises that can help you warm up your voice. They are as follows:

Stand straight and exhale all the air from your lungs and keep pushing it out until you feel like everything is out.

Once all the air has been pushed out, you will automatically start to inhale and draw in deeper breaths.

You have to visualize how the air enters your lungs, and imagine it as being food for your hungry lungs.

Keep repeating this for about three to four times.

Next, exhale the air out comfortably.

Follow it by taking in a deep breath but not pushing your limit.

Hold it in for about 15 seconds before releasing it.

Increase the holding time to 30 seconds, followed by 45 seconds and so on.

Continue to do so until you can hold your breath for an entire minute.

This exercise is carried out in order to strengthen your diaphragm and the muscles around it.

Next up, stand erect and draw in five deep breaths with an open mouth.

You will see that you are unable to do so without using your diaphragm.

Once your lungs are full, release the air through your nose and your mouth closed.

Next, let out a hearty laugh and "ha ha" as loudly as you can.

Laugh out your inhaled breath and, once everything is exhaled, quickly draw in a deep breath.

Next up, close your lips tightly and laugh through your nose without making a sound.

Your diaphragm will expand and contract accordingly.

Next up, stand straight and bend down to touch your toes.

Do not try to exert too much pressure while doing so and go down gently.

Remain still for 1 to 2 minutes.

Breathe out and go back to the erect position.

Stand straight and place your hands over your hips and push your shoulders backwards and try to look at the ceiling and yawn.

Your waist should expand and your diaphragm should inflate and deflate to let the air in and out.

Exhale the breath out to produce an "om" sound.

Next up, stand straight and draw in deep breaths and, as you release the breath, count from one to five in a single breath.

Once you are comfortable, count from one to ten in a single breath, but make sure you do not strain your vocal chords and the air moves in and out effortlessly.

Open a book and read a combination of long and short sentences within a single breath.

Remember not to fill up your lungs too much before speaking as it can make you feel uncomfortable. Your mind will always tell you when you should stop and you should listen to it. Your breath should be easy to control and keep you comfortable.

Yawning can help you release some of the tension in your neck and jaw and thus, yawn before you speak to someone just to be free.

When it comes to carrying out some of these in public, you have to be subtle about it so that people do not notice it. If you are giving a speech, then you must control your breath in such a way that the microphone does not pick up on it.

CHAPTER 4: BASICS ELEMENT OF COMMUNICATIONS

Communication is simply the transmission of information, usually between different individuals or groups. It involves:

Sender or source (the one who has the information and wants to transmit it),

Receiver (the one who receives the information),

Message (the information you want to convey)

Channel (medium through which information is delivered e.g. by telephone, by paper)

Code (set of rules that are known to the sender and receiver that are used to send the message eg language)

Feedback (response from the receiver after getting message eg a triggered emotion when receiving good/bad news)

VERBAL AND NONVERBAL COMMUNICATION

We generally refer to communication as an oral or written exchange of information. These sounds and the language used to convey a message are called verbal communication.

However, over 70% of the message is sent through non-verbal forms (tone of voice, expression, gestures, clothes, proximity to the recipient, etc.). Try to imagine what the cat in the picture is saying, "I'm so happy with this!" Is your impression the one sent verbally (if you're really happy)? Or is the nonverbal message too strong for you to believe that you are happy?

Communication is often considered to be inevitable. It is impossible not to transmit. Even if you don't say or write anything, that's behaviour, the way you dress, the way you walk and sit, it all sends a message. Even if you completely cut off yourself from the rest of the world, you still communicate, saying, "I don't want to see anyone!" What you do, how you behave, your facial expression, eye contact, and the tone of your voice, each of these elements "tells" something to the other person. And most importantly, they can all be misunderstood.

Keep in mind that it's not just what you say that matters. As you say it is sometimes more important!

THE DIMENSIONS OF COMMUNICATION

Moreover, even when we refer to verbal communication, if we spend a little time analysing the process, we will notice that whenever we communicate something, we are not just delivering a message. Take, for example, the following workplace communication between an employee and his or her superior:

It may seem simple enough: one person shows evidence that another came later. Well, this is just the fair part of the message. Going deeper into its meaning, we can see that this person is also conveying other information. First, by rebuking him, she is emphasizing that she is in a higher hierarchical position, so something is being conveyed about the relationship between the two. Secondly, by saying this, she is saying that she is not satisfied with what has happened and should not happen again, so a call to action is sent. Finally, she is also saying something about herself that she is not very tolerant of people who do not arrive on time.

What we think is just "one message" is actually 4 messages:

One objective: "I saw that you arrived late again."

A self-revelation: "I'm not happy when people arrive late!"

A call to action: "Please don't be late again!"

Something about their relationship: "I'm your boss!"

Why is it important to know these things? Well, knowing that communication is never a message and that they are conveying a lot at the same time, even if unintentional, makes us more aware of the mistakes that can happen, where they might arise and why.

Imagine that our attitude towards a colleague is neutral, and we tend not to communicate with him. Nothing bad can come of it, right? Well, not exactly! This person may interpret silence as a sign of hostility and get the impression that we do not like him, so he will behave accordingly. Basically, we did nothing wrong, but as there are many aspects involved in communication; there is now a heavy climate between us.

Thinking of another example, let's now ask an organization volunteer to bring us the stapler. Simple, right? Well, again, not exactly! Even if the message we are sending is that we need a stapler, we are also talking about our relationship. Since he is a new volunteer, you can understand from the message that, being a new member of the team, we regard him as a lower team member. And again the voltage increases without the emitter realizing why.

Let's think about something we probably all did at one point: being late for a meeting. We can get there with the best possible intentions, but that will not prevent others from thinking that the meeting is not important to us as we did not even bother to arrive on time. Even without being there, we have communicated that person (s) with something negative, and this will likely affect the next interaction.

For all these and many other aspects that have not been addressed here, it is very important indeed that in communicating we take into account all the different stages of the process and also make sure that all the messages we are sending will not be misunderstood.

Chapter 5: How to Communicate with People to Build Friendships

Let's be perfectly honest here, building lasting friendships is hard. People come in and out of your life so often that it is not easy to find one that you can keep forever. Friendship, however, is incredibly important. Friends help relieve stress, make you happier, give advice, and just generally make your life better. How do you make lasting friendships like that?

Choose Carefully

You cannot be friends with everyone. Well, maybe you could, but it is not recommended. It is best to remain acquaintances with people until you have time to 'test the waters' and see how you feel about the other person. If you feel awkward or out of place, this is probably not the person you are looking for. If you are relaxed and feel as though you are able to be yourself around this person and speak easily, then you have found a good candidate.

Honesty

The key to any relationship is to be honest and genuine. The same goes for friendship. You can't be good friends with fake people. Don't be afraid to open yourself up. Always speak the truth and be authentically yourself. When you share stories, allow your new friends to see the emotions the story causes, lay yourself out there. Does this open you up for heartache and hurt? Yes, in a way, but it also lays down a foundation of trust and compassion decent people will not be able to deny. Give your friend compliments, it is totally okay. Also, be thankful when they give you compliments, but remember to be humble and stay grounded. Remember that your friends are their own individuals, do not try to 'fix' them or change them, allow them to be themselves.

Don't Be Afraid of Silence

When speaking of communication, people assume that means you have to actually speak. This is not so. We have all heard or experienced the so-called awkward silence. The beauty of a true friendship is that there is no awkwardness in the silence. You are able to sit together and just do things quietly without feeling like you should get up and go. This kind of silence speaks volumes about trust and mutual respect. If you are lucky enough, you will build the kind of friendships in which you can communicate with just a glance or a motion. There are more ways to communicate than just through speech.

Don't Step Down

If for some reason you and your friend find yourselves at odds, do not back down. Never walk away from an argument. Take the time to calmly make your side known, careful to keep your tone level and your words small. Make clear what the problem is and how you feel about it. Then, be sure to offer your friend the same in return. Be an active listener, look them in the eye, use your body language to show that you are interested in the conversation, and do not interrupt.

Communication is a useful tool in more professional relationships as well. You can use these skills to market and network yourself to the general public in order to boost your business and get your name out.

Chapter 6: Go Public

You've been hearing the cliché "face your fear" or "conquer your fear" a gazillion times, but guess why people always say that. It's because that is the fastest way to get through it. Public speaking always involves the public, your very fear, and there is no shortcut in doing it.

Great minds are not immediately understood unless their ideas are explained clearly, simply and directly. Brilliance needs interpretation to shine through, and a public speaker needs an audience to speak to. Procrastinating facing your very fear will leave you hiding in a scary nook all your life.

To overcome public speaking fear and anxiety fast, you have to practice it in the most literal sense: speaking in public. Face people and talk with strangers. Let the public know that you are there and you need their attention without seeming needy. Take it one step at a time.

Give one-liners

Believe it or not, but one-liners are the hardest words to say. Saying "thank you very much" to a person who just gave you the right direction is hard to say in the most audible way. Saying "I'm sorry" every time you commit a mistake is as hard as accepting your fault. Saying "good morning" or "hello" to a stranger is unheard of for some people. Now, how do you expect to speak in public if you cannot utter simple words that are full of meaning?

From now on, give one-liners every time you go to the grocery, ride a bus or accidentally bump with someone. Say a warm "thank you" to the assisting cashier behind the cash register. Say "hi!" with a smile to the person sitting next to you on the bus or subway. Make it a habit to say "I'm sorry" every time you do something unintentional, harmful or not, big or small.

Responding to small things, when habitually done, becomes a natural part of you. The genuine connection and intention become inherent, so facing a crowd and getting their attention and affection becomes natural for you.

Walk down the street and count how many one-liners you can give.

Start a conversation

Chitchat if you may. A good practice to overcome your fear and anxiety of public speaking is to engage a total stranger in a conversation about anything that you think will interest that person. It doesn't matter if you want to talk about the sunset or the scheduled big film next summer.

The challenge is not really to make a sense out of your discussion, but to hold off the stranger's attention for as long as you can. Holding off attention for a longer time translates to effectiveness as a speaker.

There are natural conversationalists who can make people forget time and genuinely make them interested about things they do not really care about. These conversationalists specialize in small talks with a smaller group in a more intimate set-up. They are the best candidates for a public speaker because great things start small. If you cannot capture a few people's attention, how do you expect to engage a huge crowd?

Talk to a stranger next to you in a café, and pretend to ask for a recommendation on the menu. Speak with a stranger at the train station and pretend to ask for direction. If you see someone who has the same interest as yours, say, a hobby at the park or fashion statement, start a conversation about your common ground.

The trick here is looking at the same direction, meeting on the same page and heeding instead of listening.

Make arguments

Making people agree or disagree is the first sign of persuasion, and persuasion is the real power of speaking. To unleash this key, see if you can get people to share the same thoughts as yours or get them blurt out their opposing opinions.

Make them nod. Make them laugh or frown. Make them ask questions. You can even make them mad not by offending them but by showing a strong position that they may not agree with. Arousing people's emotions is a gift that the best public speakers possess.

If you will succeed with this exercise, it will be the confirmation of your strong delivery, clear explanation, absolute connection and sheer sensitivity.

Join groups with the same intention

Fear and anxiety of public speaking is a problem that millions of people experience. You are not the only one in this battle. Join forum groups and speech organizations to guide you closely towards achieving your goal.

Toastmasters International is the most-known non-profit organization that helps people build confidence and learn public speaking from the core. It has produced politicians, businessmen and motivational speakers in the past, and you might be the next one.

Chapter 7: YOUR IMAGE

Image is the set of beliefs and associations held by the public that receives direct or indirect communications from people, products or services, brands, companies or organizations.

Image has its origin in the Latin -imāgo- and allows us to describe the figure, representation, similarity, aspect or appearance of a certain thing.

2.1.- DECISIONS

83% of decisions are made by the eyes. Think about how we react quickly when we see something: a person, a place or a any other thing and immediately decide if we want it for ourselves or not, causing as a consequence our action of acceptance or rejection. It is not uncommon for one of the most popular sayings to be "Love is born of sight", because the eyes and the sense of sight are the conduit through which most stimuli enter us. Remember how it was that we decided to buy a tie or the earrings that we wear; how we choose the person with whom we have a romantic relationship, well ... how we even evaluate whether a restaurant its of our like or not without even having tasted its food. .. by the eyes. The sense of sight is so important in our decisions that in some cases it comes to replace other senses that should be determined in the first place. That happens when they bring us a very well presented dish and before trying it we say: "Mmm ... How delicious it looks! ... when we should say ..." Mmm ..., how delicious it tastes! ... ", once we would have tried that dish, which would be more logical, but it is not like that.

The lesson is that from now on we must give more importance to all the visual stimuli that we emit, no matter if we are people or institutions.

2.2.- STIMULUS

The brain process that decodes the stimuli takes a few seconds, the scientists do not agree, some say five seconds and there are those who consider up to twelve. It does not matter, the fact is that, it is the first seconds that constitute the critical moment in which we make a first impression. Americans say: "First impressions, last impressions" and we know that, "The first impression is the one that counts", because that is the one that is going to remain engraved in the mind of the one who perceives us for the first time.

How many times have we been misinterpreted because they met us at a time when we felt bad, angry or sleepy because we had to work through the night and gave the impression of being bored, lazy or aggressive? Next time we will need to think about the consequences of causing a bad first impression, because otherwise it will be very difficult to make people change their mind.

2.3.- FEELINGS

The mind decides mostly based on feelings, it is still common to find a large number of businessmen or politicians who reject the important role played by emotions in the world of decision making. They still believe that people think with their brains and that deciding is a rational process based on logic. Therefore they try to convince with long arguments full of many considerations that must be stopped and deeply analyzed by their audience. Pity ... they do not even know that the time that people are willing to listen without distraction is seven minutes, otherwise something has to happen to get their attention back. Studies by two medical researchers in the San Francisco area have uncovered evidence to prove that some functions of the brain, especially those that refer to decision-making skills, are governed more by emotions than by reason.

Doctors David Sobel and Robert Ornstein, neurologists at the University of California Medical Center, have identified a command center within the brain that controls our decisions, functions and talents, so let them be the ones to tell us their conclusions: " We would like a rational and judicious component of the human brain to control this range of talents, unfortunately for those who think this way, and fortunately for the survival of the organism, the mental operating system of control and command is more intimately linked with emotions and automatic defense systems that with reason and conscious thought, we have a brain that operates much more with emotions than with reason ".

From a few years ago until this date, a scientific model of the emotional mind has emerged that explains how much of what we do can be directed emotionally and how emotions have their own logic. Two of the best scientific studies in this regard have been commanded separately by Paul Ekman, head of the Human Interaction Laboratory at the University of California, San Francisco, and by clinical psychologist at the University of Massachusetts Seymour Epstein. Both point to a series of qualities that distinguish emotions from the rest of mental activities. The emotional mind is much faster than the rational mind that requires more time for reflection and cold analysis. The emotional mind decides and puts into action the rest of the body without stopping to think about what and why it is doing something. However, the actions that arise from the emotional mind carry a very strong sense of certainty as a consequence of a simple and simplified way of seeing things that can be absolutely disconcerting for the rational mind. The time between the stimulus that activates the emotion and the unchaining of it, is calculated in brain time as thousandths of a second and the need to act is so fast that it does not enter into consciousness. Of course, sometimes this rapid mode of perception sacrifices the accuracy in favor of the speed of the action, but on the other hand it has the benefit that it can interpret an emotional reality in an instant, emitting intuitive value judgments that indicate the best way of reacting to a stimulus. Since the rational mind takes more time than the emotional mind to register and respond, the initiative in an emotional situation will take the heart not the head. It is kind of an emotional radar that will indicate the best way forward with the only drawback that sometimes intuitive judgments can be wrong or false, but fortunately it is the minority of cases.

In general, human beings decide based 85% on their feelings and only 15% on their thoughts, after a cold and long analysis. It is true that we usually use facts to justify a decision we want to make, but finally we end up deciding what our heart dictates. If it weren't for the heart, billions of dollars would not be sold worldwide for image-based products. Studies show that automobiles are purchased based on style and color above the most sophisticated mechanical considerations. We simply buy a car because we like it and that's it. We all know that a clock gives us the time with the same efficiency as a Rolex. So what is it that justifies spending thousands of dollars more? ... emotions ... simply the emotions that a Rolex can makes us feel.

2.4.- POWER OF INFLUENCE

A better image, greater power of influence and having a good image reports among many other benefits: increase in self-confidence, increase in the level of confidence transmitted and, what is more important: attainment of credibility, so that it will optimize the overall performance in a competed global scenario. That is, having a good public image grants power and provides an ADDED VALUE to the brand, institution or person, which translates into having more weapons to be able to convince the target group that we are the best at something in order to obtain and maintain their preference.

CHAPTER 8: What's YOUR Story?

For the techniques in this book to be effective, it's important that you become very clear on exactly **how** you experience your communication challenge – what's the story you tell yourself about it? The best way to begin uncovering all the aspects of your problem is to simply free write about it (preferably the old-fashioned way – by hand with pen and paper). Keep it casual and remember that this is completely private – you're having a conversation with yourself. Write as much as you can (at least a full page) about this issue, in as dramatic a fashion as you can without censoring yourself in any way. This document represents the soon-to-be ancient history of you as a presenter. The more you write, the more your subconscious programming will be revealed. So get relaxed, find a quiet space and let loose! Feel free to audio record yourself speaking the story, then transcribe it onto paper, if that seems an easier way to unload your baggage.

Now embellish your epic of sorrow with the following details. We want to get all

of your anxiety-provoking cards on the table.

How long it has been going on – what's your first memory of this being a problem? What do you say to yourself about this in your head? Maybe you've labeled yourself as small, inept, incomplete – or even something really mean, like 'loser'. What is the MOST fearful part about presenting? It might be:

☐ Walking up to the podium
☐ Hearing yourself being introduced
☐ Remembering what to say in the first few moments of the talk - anticipating a mental blackout
☐ Looking out into the audience – what facial expressions do you expect?

- The Q&A session – having to think on your feet
- Knowing that you **appear** nervous to your audience – shaky voice, sweating, speaking too fast, etc.

What do you dread most about preparing beforehand?

- The anticipation of feeling anxious in the weeks and days and hours beforehand – loss of sleep, unfocused at work, etc.
- Outlining the content / Preparing the slides
- Rehearsing the lines / script
- Sitting amongst the audience at the big event, awaiting your turn to be 'on'

What kind of audience or performance triggers the strongest reaction?

- Peer groups, colleagues
- Authority figures – supervisors, experts, people you admire
- Technical or complicated informational presentations
- Sales pitches to prospective clients
- Singing, being uniquely expressive

☐ Sharing personal information in public

Conversely, are there groups of people you feel really comfortable 'performing' for? These might include:
☐ Joke telling at a dinner among friends
☐ Taking charge of an extended family drama
☐ Storytelling at a school classroom
☐ Teaching young people, training junior level colleagues
☐ Offering spiritual guidance at a place of worship

Recognizing that you are comfortable communicating in some situations – i.e. you're already a successful performer – is a powerful part of yourself to draw upon in this work.

What's your best theory about why this is a problem for YOU? Whatever you believe strongly tends to manifest as personal truth, so take a look at how you've labeled this problem for yourself. You might say things like:
"I'm naturally shy, introverted – always

have been, always will be"
"I have stage fright"

"I just can't express myself well with words"
"Other people always intimidate me"
"I'm not good at thinking on my feet"
"It's egotistical and arrogant to even **want** to be in the spotlight"

HOW do you know it's a problem for you? Many of us who have suffered with this challenge do an excellent job of hiding it from the world. And yet YOU know you have it. But HOW do you know you have it, exactly?

Close your eyes and bring to mind the picture of standing up in front of an audience. Let the usual anxiety kick in (just pretend). Where do you feel it inside your body – does it have a color, a weight, a pressure, a structure, a texture? Some people feel this as a weight on their chest, holding them back; others describe feeling they are surrounded by walls, or held back by a net. Maybe it's sheer panic, like a blackout.

While you may go to great lengths to avoid conjuring up the sensations of discomfort that public speaking brings up, simply knowing that our imagination can re-create the symptoms **reassures us that we can tap into that same** power to dissolve them

The way in which you hold onto this problem inside of you will be unique to you – there is no wrong, or abnormal way to sense it. Write down whatever pops into your head first. Oftentimes the first thought is the best (i.e. correct) thought. Finally, fill in these blanks. My general attitude and mood about presenting is _____. For me to be effective and dynamic I would have to be _____ and do

_____

_____

         and   have

_____

.

Go back now and re-read everything you've written. Did anything surprise you? A lot of what we believe remains hidden from our awareness until we do a deep spring cleaning of the subconscious. Look over the words you chose. Were there many absolutes (**never, always**) or extreme feelings (**hatred, terror**)? Highlight with pen or mouse those strong words together with any unusually negative, self-defeating terms. You will come back to this story later in the program.

Use your story to fill up the Issue Deconstruction Diagram below. You will find it a useful tool to return to and chart your progress as all of these aspects of the issue gradually dissolve.

ISSUE DECONSTRUCTION DIAGRAM

Chapter 9: Speaking 101

On the off chance that you need to be an actual expert open speaker, you should finish two things: (1) take in the abilities to end up element in front of an audience, and (2) transform your skill into subjects that get bookings. It's that basic ... furthermore, it's that confounded.

Regardless of the fact that you turn into an open incredible speaker, be that as it may, it isn't sufficient. Your discourse subject must offer something of genuine worth to your audience members, and it should be something that individuals will pay to hear and learn.

On the off chance that you need to profit as an open speaker, the primary thing you have to do is make a rundown of what you know. What learning and abilities have you created throughout the years that could be of assistance to a unique number of individuals? What do you realize that others have to know?

Give Your Gathering of people an Advantage

Your theme must have a particular advantage for your crowd, and your title must make that position clear. Appealing is essential, yet don't lose the power. "The Force of Positive Considering" may not be the world's most sharp title, but rather the group of onlookers knows precisely what they're going to get. Never give up clarity for astuteness.

You additionally should be precise and particular about your real business sector. Make a rundown of associations or organizations that could most utilize your mastery. Ensure you're putting forth them something they require. If you aren't certain how helpful your attitude may be, get your work done. Perused relevant articles, and research the points of different speakers.

Make a Press Unit

With a specific end goal to profit as an expert speaker, you should to either enlist an advertising delegate or turn into your best supporter. This includes advertising. You're calling card will be your "press pack," which ought to incorporate an expert photo of yourself, data about your points, your bio, testimonials or letters of suggestion, reprints of articles you've composed, a video of a talking engagement, and any media clippings and public statements.

Obviously, in case you're simply beginning, you may need to make a "sham" video. You needn't present a whole discourse in the video, however, ensure it looks proficient. What's more, dependably send a customized introductory letter with your press unit!

Other than your physical press pack, you will require a site to serve as your "online media group." Add gushing video to your web page, and make a business card with your website address.

The Force of Systems Administration

Systems management is inherently imperative. Give out your business card, and direct individuals to your site. Tell everybody you meet that you're a speaker, and get them amped up for your points. Inquire as to whether they know any individual who might be intrigued. Give them 2 or 3 of your business cards, and request that they pass them along. If you can allude somebody to every individual's business, take an additional business card of theirs also. Apparently, catch up and do as you guarantee, staying in contact with the general population you meet.

Initially, you will probably need to get the majority of your bookings yourself. Speaker's dressers and specialists more often than not work just with speakers who have a long reputation. Make contacts at whatever point conceivable, and send your press unit to your prospects. Make something free that your new prospects can arrange from your site, or encase a postpaid return postcard with your press pack. You can offer a little booklet with data applicable to your theme or a Compact disc containing a short Powerpoint presentation. The general population who request your free blessing will turn into your top prospects. Follow up with them to get bookings.

Chapter 10: Basic Simple Speech Structure

Everything should be made as simple as possible, but not simpler. – Albert Einstein

The easiest and quickest way to write and give a short, simple speech is to apply the KISS system. Keep It Simple, Sweetheart.

Most speeches can easily follow this format:

~Tell them what you are going to tell them;

~Tell them;

~Tell them what you told them.

Simple, eh?

This method is the easiest for beginners to start with because it can be adapted to any speech. It is also easy to remember.

Let`s look at that list again:

~Introduction: Tell them what you are going to tell them; ask a question or pose a problem.

~Body: Tell them; present points and supporting information

~Conclusion: Tell them what you told them; summarize your main points.

Combine that with writing your speech in point form, rehearsing it multiple times and you can write a speech right now if you wanted to.

If done right, it will be hard to tell where the introduction, body, and conclusion begin and end. One will flow naturally into the other.

In the rest of this book, we will expand on this simple concept further.

Summary

Tell them what you are going to tell them;

Tell them;

Tell them what you told them.

Speech Introduction

All speech, written or spoken, is a dead language, until it finds a willing and prepared hearer. - Robert Louis Stevenson

In line with what the quote above says, the purpose of an introduction is to create "a willing and prepared hearer." A good introduction grabs the audience's interest and tells them what you will be presenting. It gets them eager to hear your speech.

Have you ever attended a speech where you did not care about it? Perhaps you did not relate to the topic and saw no need to listen. Worse, perhaps you had no idea what the speech was about at all. This is likely due to a poorly constructed introduction.

Worse, have you ever been the speaker giving a speech that the audience did not listen to?

By just doing one simple thing, you can easily pique the interest of your audience.

It is a simple way of "Telling them what you are going to tell them."

Here are a few ways to have a good opening:

~A question

~A situation, story or illustration

~A challenging statement

~A quotation

~Displaying a picture

~Presenting a visual aid, such as an object or instrument

~A generalization that grabs the audience's attention

The simplest way to arouse interest is to ask a question that catches the interest of the audience.

To get the audience interested, mention a problem the audience has or arouse their curiosity about something.

Example - How Problems can be Blessings

One example is how problems can actually be blessings. This type of speech does well in a Toastmaster meeting. The completely written speech is in the Appendix.

"Have you ever had an embarrassing moment that turned out to be a blessing in disguise?"

Many people will say to themselves, "Never!" They will wonder how embarrassment could end up being a good thing.

Example - Hotel Giving Outstanding Customer Service

Another example is a hotel that wants to stay at the forefront of giving outstanding customer service. The completely written speech is in the Appendix.

"How can we find out how to make our customers even happier? Our traditional customer survey is good, but what about things not covered in our customer survey? How do we find out what the customer wants when they may not be fully aware of it?"

This will get the listeners wondering, "How do we find out what a customer wants when even they are not aware of what they want? Is that even possible?"

Example - Engineer Recommending a Policy Change

Our third example is about an electronic product that has a problem; too many units are coming back for repair. This is expensive and an Engineer named Fred has a solution. Here is how he might introduce his presentation to management and Senior Engineers. The completely written speech is in the Appendix.

"Using a simple and well-known circuit design technique, our repair costs will plummet, the quality of our electronic products will increase and our customers will be happier."

Who does not want to see costs plummet? Happier customers are always a good thing. Since management often thinks in terms of money and customer base, this will get their attention.

Notice that these introductions do not tell the audience what the answer is. The purpose of an introduction is only one thing: to get your audience to want to listen to what you have to say. They have to listen to the rest of the speech to find out.

How Long Should The Introduction Be?

That depends on the length of the entire speech. For a 5-7 minute speech, the introduction should take less than a minute. The introduction should flow naturally into the body of the speech so that it is hard to notice where the introduction starts and the body begins.

For longer speeches, the introduction may be several minutes. For very short speeches, the introduction will be almost non-existent.

Some speeches are literally 90 seconds. Start-up companies pitch angel investors in Vancouver with 90-second presentations. The introduction usually consists of "Hi, we are [company name] and we make [product]. We are looking for [money/a mentor/etc.]."

Then they quickly present an overview of what they do and what they want (this is the body of their speech). If they pique the interest of enough investors, they are invited back to give a much longer presentation.

Memorize the First Few Sentences

Most speakers are nervous when they begin speaking. This makes it easy to forget the words you need to say to rivet your listeners' attention. Yet the first few sentences grab your audience's attention. How do you ensure you will not mess this up?

One simple technique will ensure your introduction starts out exactly as you intended it to be.

Simply write down the first few sentences of your introduction and memorize them word for word. Go over them until you can recite them from memory no matter how nervous you are.

I prefer to go a step further and completely memorize my introduction word for word totally. This way I do not forget it and it has the exact impact I want it to have.

Of course, this works well for 5-7 minute speeches because then the introduction is only a few sentences long.

A four-hour speech will have a much longer introduction. In that case, I still commit the first two or three sentences to memory. The rest of the introduction is written in point form.

Summary

The purpose of a speech introduction is to tell your audience what you will be talking about and motivating them to listen to the rest of the speech.

Tell them what you are going to tell them.

Introduce a topic by asking a question or posing a problem the audience has. Make them wonder what the solution might be.

Alternatively, you can use a quotation or a display of some kind.

Arouse the audience's curiosity about the speech topic.

The introduction does not answer the question it poses; the rest of the speech does that.

Write down and memorize the first few sentences in your introduction. This will prevent memory lapses during your initial nervousness and your introduction can start out with a bang.

Chapter 11: YOUR AUDIENCE'S HIDDEN SECRET, REVEALED

Your audience has something they have not been telling you. You are scared to death to present, and they are keeping secrets. That's cruel, isn't it? Don't worry. I am going to tell you their secret.

In Section One, we discussed the three ways to "POP" your fear of public speaking. The invitation to address an audience of any size is nothing more than a request for you to share what you have learned. Your expertise, knowledge, wisdom, and story is valuable to those who gathered to hear you speak. You are their teacher. You are their trainer. But there is something they are not telling you. It's their best kept secret. Are you ready for the secret? Here it is.

Your audience wants you to succeed.

They want you to do well. They want you to awe them, wow them, and teach them. Think about the last time you attended a presentation. Did you sit in your seat and have an internal conversation that sounded like, "I hope this man or woman totally messes up. I hope they bomb!"?

I doubt it. You wanted to learn, to be inspired, to be moved to do better in your business or life. Your audiences are the same. They want you to succeed. The more you succeed, the more they learn. What a relief.

Still not convinced this is true? As a communications coach, presenters hire me to watch them give public speaking remarks. I sit in the back, take copious notes, and share feedback with them at the conclusion of their presentation. I tell them what was strong and ways they could improve their future performance. In most cases, the presentations go as planned. On a handful of occasions, however, I've witnessed presenters fail. These folks bombed. Bad! In one case, the speaker forgot his remarks and remained silent for 2 minutes. Another person physically fell down, flat on his face.

In each of these "disaster" cases, the speakers recovered. Within a few minutes, they were back into their speech. As you can imagine, the speakers left the stage horrified at the conclusion of their presentation. They never wanted to speak in front of a crowd again. Ever. They thought they blew it. The audience feedback and reviews, on the other hand, suggested otherwise. To his surprise, the man who fell on his face received comments like, "That was one of the best speeches I have ever heard" and "Incredible content." The gentleman who forgot his remarks for the first two minutes of his speech was delighted to read, "Public speaking is hard, and I think we can all relate to being nervous at the beginning of a big speech."

You are not the only one who feels and recognizes the challenges of public speaking. Take the stage with a higher level of ease knowing your audience understands your struggle and wants you to do great. That alone should bring you peace of mind, confidence, and a desire to serve the crowd. The same crowd that wants your success just as much as you do.

CHAPTER 12: Focus Your Speech on the Audience Expectations

Before you get into practicing your public speaking skills, the first thing you need to do is understand the actual audience that you will be presenting.

For example, if you're giving a persuasive speech to a bunch of retirees on business investments in the morning, you would prepare the speech significantly different if you were speaking again in the afternoon about business investments to a group of newlyweds.

You should always research and prepare your speech based on the audience that you're going to be delivering it to.

Speaking to a group of elderly people, you would speak slower, with much more focused facts, and talk about shorter-term investment strategies. When speaking with the newlyweds, you deliver a faster cadence, perhaps more socially focused on careers and earning income over a longer period of time.

Use basic common sense when it comes to preparation for your speech. You want to also focus on hot button issues that the particular group that you're speaking with, would be very interested to hear. Another example would be discussing Social Security and how it impacts retirement and investments to the elderly. If you were speaking to a younger crowd you may only gloss over this point. See how important it is to have the right focus?

Using Your Strengths

to Really Deliver

An audience is going to be significantly more interested in what you have to say, if you have expertise as well is the ability to overrate your expertise in a manner that is interesting and stimulating as well as entertaining and educational.

This is why you should use your strengths when delivering a powerful and engaging speech. Utilizing your strengths means that you also develop your own speaking style which can propel you in your career and the ability to continue to move upward in society.

You should not focus on delivering speeches counter intuitive to your personality. For example, if you are by nature a bit of a jokester, giving a solemn speech may not be the best utilization of your talents.

Of course sometimes, we have to give a speech that may require us to remain focused on the right kind of skills and delivering what the audience is expecting to hear.

Another example is that you would not necessarily crack jokes at a funeral; of course there are always exceptions to this rule, but understanding the audience expectations is the first and most important focus to allow you to then mash your personality with the kind of speech that you will need to create.

Understand the Kind of Speech You Need To Present

In order to develop content expertise you must first understand the kind of speech that you need to present.

This is why research of your audience and then focusing on hot button issues and points of interest that your audience wants to know about, is absolutely critical to understand.

Once you understand the audience, next you must decide on the exact kind of speech:

Informative – This speech delivers content that people can then be shaped or molded into accepting or at least considering.

Persuasive – This is the kind of speech most people imagine; where you have to convince a group / people to see things from your point of view.

Special occasion – This speech is often used to commemorate an event such as a wedding where family members and/or friends toast the event.

Passionate Speech – Something you feel strongly about and how you would share your passion with others.

There are of course, other types of public speaking but these are the four most common and for beginners this is where you should focus your attention.

CHAPTER 13: MAKE OUT AN OUTLINE

Remember our assumption, that you have something interesting to share. You have researched the topic, updating your material with the latest information available. Likely, you gathered more materials than you can realistically hope to use within the time allotted for your talk. Therefore, decision has to be made as to what to use, when and how. To be able to follow your decisions, you need a working outline.

When you set out to build a house or any other physical structure, you readily see the need to prepare a plan. It is unusual to start your house without a thoughtful drawing. A good working drawing would show exactly where each facility in the building would be placed.

Your speech outline plays a similar role. It helps you to organise your thoughts so that the delivery would flow smoothly, transiting from one segment to another in a certain order, or a predetermined sequence.

The size of your outline would depend on the length of the talk. While a short talk may require no more than a mental outline of how to proceed, or a few jottings on a small piece of paper, a full hour lecture would call for a full page written outline. Otherwise, there's possibility of omitting important details, or getting things jumbled up and sounding illogical or incoherent.

No matter the length of your speech, you do well to shun the usual urge by rookie speakers to write down every detail of their talk in long, unwieldy, manuscript, which is then read out word for word. Reading from a manuscript gives you away as green horn. A speaker cannot sound natural or conversational while burying his face on the pages of a bulky manuscript. It even says to the audience, 'hey, this guy does not know what he's talking about!'

Points to note

Keep it simple

The outline does not need to be complicated or loaded with too much details. Like any other skeleton, it shows only the bones, not the flesh. The meat of your talk would be supplied during the actual delivery.

Keep it organised

It is your judgement call to determine how you intend to marshal out your points. You may adopt a chronological presentation, if the subject allows it, treating the issues in their sequence of occurrence. Or you may organise them according to themes and supporting evidences. In any case, the ideas must follow in some sort of logical order, with appropriate connectives leading from one point to another.

Experienced speakers find it useful to keep repeating the theme of their talk at intervals. If you choose to follow this good practice, it would be helpful to indicate in the outline, where the reminders would occur.

Stick to the outline

Yes, you have an outline to guide you. But there's always the temptation to stray during delivery. You could veer off the outline and begin to dwell on items that you deliberately left out while selecting the points to use. Dwelling on such points could make you overlook some important details or push your talk overtime.

CHAPTER 14: How to get rid of the fear of public speaking using these proven techniques

Fear of speaking is a major concern for most public speakers. Certain fear is a good thing. It gives you energy which makes your talk good. However, there is also a bad fear. One that makes your mind go blank on stage. This is a fear you need to avoid. So how can you do it?

There are a number of highly effective ways. Use them all and you should find your fear will disappear.

What is the main reason why you have this fear? It's because you care about what your audience will think of you. You fear that your talk will not be good enough. You fear ridicule.

Think about this for a moment. This is also the fear that makes people introverts.

They fear what people will think of them. They don't have the confidence to know that they are good enough. They are frightened to mix in because they care about what people will think of them.

The false belief that causes fear

So how do you overcome this fear? You need to remember why you are giving your talk. Remember your main goal you read about earlier. You have information that will improve their lives. You know things that they don't. Things that they want to know. You have an edge. They should listen to you because of this. By remembering this fact, you should know that instead of ridiculing you, they will be thanking and praising you. You are there to help them.

Is this the cure for fear of public speaking? It certainly helps, but there are several things you should do.

Tell them

When you first go on stage be honest with your audience. Simply tell them that you're scared to death of coming on stage. Or something like that. Why?

When you tell them that you are fearful, they will totally understand. They will know that it must be daunting to get up on that stage.

What this does, is that it gets them on your side. This is a very effective but simple thing. Just by telling your audience how nervous you are, seems to have a calming effect. You will probably get a laugh from the audience. Not laughing at you, but laughing with you.

Make a big thing out of it. Go up there and say something like, "I'm actually petrified to come up here. My bones are almost shattering with the trembling". This will more than likely get a laugh and break the ice with you and your audience. When this happens, you will likely find your nerves settle down quite a lot.

Next time you are up on stage, try it. You will find it a wonderful ice-breaker and will have an immediate relaxing effect on you.

What to do beforehand

There is something you should be doing before every public speaking event.

Years ago, I worked for this company where I was attending a management training course. Part of the training involved learning how to give training sessions. So naturally, we had to learn how to stand up and give a presentation in front of our colleagues. We were all allowed a day to prepare.

The next day we had all prepared our talk on a subject chosen by the trainer.

This one particular young fellow stood up and gave his five minute presentation. It was all about his holiday in Vegas.

His presentation was brilliant. We all thought that he must be already very experienced. He was so confident throughout.

We were all wrong. It turned out that this was his first talk. He actually admitted he was very nervous. You wouldn't think it; he looked very confident.

What was his secret?

It was very simple. He had rehearsed in front of a mirror at home. He gave the presentation to himself three to five times. Why was this so effective?

Rehearsing in this way is like a dry run. It's how fire drills work.

When there is no actual danger, you are relaxed. Your mind is clear and you are able to perform without fear. You can think clearly.

What happens is that this calmness carries over to when there is a real emergency. That's why fire drills work.

By having several dry runs, when there isn't any pressure, you will find that the calmness is still there when you come to give the actual talk. It works like magic. I strongly advise you to try it.

Don't try to rehearse your talk word-for-word. Doing this will make your talk stifled and robotic. Never a good thing. I'll expand on this a lot more when you learn about the best ways to plan your talk.

Who to copy

Who should you copy to be more relaxed? The answer is no one.

You should be yourself.

Trying to be like someone else, will make it hard for you. You will also not come over in the best possible way.

Here is what I mean.

A while ago I started creating video information products. Essentially; how to videos.

It involved talking while recording a video of what I was showing on my computer screen. I had been inspired by other successful video product creators. Their videos were great and I wanted mine to be as good.

I admired one particular person. I absolutely loved his videos. One thing I noticed was his energetic way of teaching. I wanted to be like that. I thought that I needed to be like him in order to have video products that were as good.

I then started watching video products created by others. Not all of them were great. However, some were.

One person, in particular, had video courses that I also enjoyed watching. However, this person was not the same flamboyant person that the previous man was. However, the video product was still very good.

I was missing the point. What made the videos good was the content and the way it was taught. I had confused this with the style of the speaker.

I came to realise that each person were just being themselves. Yet their videos were very good.

When I realised this, I relaxed. I knew that I could just be myself. Warts and all. I stopped worrying about how I talked and even if I stuttered. I realised that just being me was good enough.

What a difference this made to my next video. I was just myself and spoke in just the same way as I would to someone face to face. I was totally relaxed. My videos products actually improved and were received much better by my customers.

The take away from this, is that you are just fine the way you are. Relax. It's OK to talk the way you normally do. Warts and all. When you just talk as yourself, you will be seen as a person just like them. Your audience will warm to you. Also, it will convey sincerity which is very important.

I would say this is one of the most powerful secrets of public speaking. Just this one thing alone will free you from the fear of public speaking. You will just go out there and talk like you would to a friend.

The unknown

Fear of the unknown will also contribute to your fear on the day. Here is some really good advice that some public speakers follow. It works.

My advice is to arrive early before anyone arrives. Test the equipment. You don't want to find that something doesn't work in the middle of your talk. Test the computer is working and the screen projector. Test the sound equipment.

Walk around the platform. Have a stroll around the room. Familiarise yourself with your surroundings.

A really good tip is to sit in different parts of the room. It will allow you to see the platform from the audience's viewpoint. Sit at each side of the room. At the back and the front. Sit in the middle.

All this may seem pointless. However, some top speakers always follow this routine because they know it works.

Finally, when people start to arrive, it's a good idea to welcome them. By doing this, you will become familiar with some of the audience members. These people will become your allies. When delivering your talk, you can pick out these people to look at when talking. It will relax you.

To summarise

Healthy butterflies are normal and can give you that edge. However, you don't want paralysing fear.

Follow the tips given and you will definitely feel a lot more relaxed.

Chapter 15: How to Write Effective and Engaging Speeches

While excellent presentation skills are necessary to successful public speaking, you also need to put a lot of focus on what you will be saying. You may be entertaining and engaging, but your audience came to the event for a reason. You want to be able to meet their expectations when it comes to the content of what you will be presenting.

Preparing your speech is integral in ensuring that the experience will be beneficial for everybody involved. A well written address should have relevant information. In addition, you need to ensure that what you prepared is sufficient for the length of time it has been slated for. Below are some useful reminders to help you write your speech:

Know Your Audience – Before you sit down and start composing a speech, it is important for you to get to know your audience first. How much background information do they have about the subject of your speech? How much do they need to know about the topic? What sort of style will they respond to? If you will be talking about saving the environment, what examples would they be able to relate to?

A speech for high school students should be written differently from one that will be used with college undergrads. In order for you to be able to relay your message effectively, you need to make sure your audience can identify with what you say.

If you will be doing a technical presentation, then it would be beneficial for you to consider the experience of your participants. It will tell you how you should write your speech to ensure that your speech is tailor fit for the people who will be sitting in your audience.

Identify Your Purpose – You were asked to speak for a reason. You need to keep this reason in mind when writing your material. What is it that your audience needs to know or learn from what you will be saying? Whether you will be doing a presentation on effective sales techniques or making toast at an anniversary dinner, your speech has a purpose. By remembering this integral element, you can create something that your audience will find relevant. You can reduce the risk of people walking out or getting bored. For example, if you will be making a toast for a newly-wed couple, then your speech needs to focus on the bliss of married life rather than talking about your college days.

Research and Brainstorming – Deciding on what to include in your speech may be a challenge at times. Even if the topic or subject you have been asked to speak about was specific, it is still up to you to figure out what you will be focusing on. For example, something as simple as making a speech at a wedding is not as easy as it sounds. If you were the best man and had to talk about the happy couple, how much information can you share without opening a can of worms? You have probably heard a few disastrous toasts where the best man accidentally talked about a past relationship or an embarrassing moment for the couple. This is, of course, something that you would want to avoid.

Creating an Outline – Once you have decided on what needs to be said in your speech, it is time to organize the information so it has a smooth flow. Some speeches tend to be confusing when the information is not arranged in a logical manner. If you were asked to introduce a guest speaker at an event, citing that person's achievements would be an important part of your introduction. The best way to present these achievements would be in chronological order. You can do it either by the year these were received or by importance.

Take Note of the Time Limit – Before sitting down to plan and build your outline, it would be beneficial to remember how long your speech is supposed to last. You will need to keep this in mind while writing your speech. In order to ensure that you stay within the time limit, you will need to take note of the word count.

The average rate of speech is about 125-150 words per minute. For the audience to understand you better, it would be ideal to stay at the bottom of that range. Anything faster will make you sound rushed or nervous. Preparing a long speech may not give you sufficient time to deliver it within the time limit.

One other thing you need to take note of is how to manage your time for speeches that last longer than thirty minutes. Talking straight for that long will not only exhaust you but your listeners as well.

Also, you want to start factoring in any visual aids that you will be using during your presentation. Remember that you will need to give the audience time to read what you have on your slides or touch the prop you will be using. So that needs to be factored in while you prepare to write.

Attention Grabbing Opening - The first few seconds of your speech is crucial. It dictates whether your audience will listen or simply sit through your entire presentation thinking about what else they would rather be doing. There are various speech hooks you can use:

Startling or Shocking Statements – Grab the attention of your audience by starting off with a statement that either shocks or piques their interest. Franklin D. Roosevelt used this technique in his speech about the Pearl Harbor Bombing. He opened with "Yesterday, December 7th, 1941 -- a date which will live in infamy -- the United States of America was suddenly and deliberately attacked by naval and air forces of the Empire of Japan."

Question – When you start your presentation with a question, you hook the audience into listening to the rest of your speech. If you were doing a presentation on improving sales skills you can begin with questions like "How much can you earn this quarter?" or "How much would you like to write on your own paycheck?" Choose questions that your audience would want to hear.

Humor or Joke – Laughter is a great ice breaker. It helps you and your audience feel relaxed with each other. So store up on those knock knocks and other wholesome jokes. However, you may want to avoid jokes that may come across as discriminating like ones that make fun of race, physical features, and religion.

Story – This type of opening engages the audience immediately. General Douglas Mac Arthur made use of it in his Sylvanus Thayer Award acceptance address. He started his speech with this, "As I was leaving the hotel this morning, a doorman asked me, "Where are you bound for, General?" And when I replied, "West Point," he remarked, "Beautiful place. Have you ever been there before?"

Personal Experience – When you start off by sharing a personal story, your audience is able to connect with you. Russell Cowell opened one of his famous speeches with "When going down the Tigris and Euphrates rivers many years ago with a party of English travelers, I found myself under the direction of an old Arab guide whom we hired up at Baghdad,"

Famous Quote – Opening with a quote from a famous personality that your audience is familiar with will get them interested in listening much sooner. If you are doing a motivational talk about perseverance quotes like this japans proverb, "Fall seven times and stand up eight" will come in handy.

Sound Effect – If you want a quick way to grab the attention of a busy audience, sound effects work like a charm. For example, if you were doing a speech on making investments, you can try knocking on your lectern and following it with "Did you hear that? That, my friends is opportunity knocking." It may sound cheesy but it surely will get your audience listening.

Statistics – Numbers are impressive and they are a sure fire way of getting your audience interested to hear more. They show that you are not just pulling your speech out from nowhere and that you have facts to back up your statements.

Developing the Body – Your speech has three integral parts, the opening, the body and the closing. The middle part is where the meat is. This is where all the necessary information is put in. In order to make it a successful public speaking experience, you will need to ensure that you develop the body of your speech properly. Here are some key points to remember:

Give it a structure that will make it easy for your audience to understand. Techniques such as acronyms or shape association help to guide your listeners through the context of what you are relaying.

Write in the same tone as you talk. Keep in mind that you will be delivering the speech and not printing it out for others to read. In addition, your personality is part of your appeal as a speaker, so make sure you do not lose it by adopting an alien tone. While it is recommended that you observe other speakers to improve your technique, morphing into their clone is not advisable.

Choose your words carefully. Great speeches go down in history because they were easy to remember and they had an impact on the listeners. One example is Franklin Roosevelt's Declaration of War in 1941. His speech originally started with "This is a day which will live in world history." However, as he delivered it, Roosevelt changed "world history" to "infamy." Up to today, that line is embedded in the hearts and minds of millions of Americans.

This does not mean that you should choose ambiguous or uncommon words to express your idea. It simply means, look for the right ones that convey the message you want to relay. Alliteration and word rhyme can be factors that you can consider when looking for the best words to use.

Being a native speaker does not guarantee that you know all the words in your language. So, use a thesaurus or dictionary to help you with this task. You may be surprised at how many options you have when it comes to words that best express or describe your idea.

Be concise to create more impact. If you have ever had to listen to a joke that has way too many details, then you would definitely appreciate this tip. By the time the speaker gets to the punch line, you get so confused that it is no longer funny. Statistics show that adults only retain 30% of what they hear. So if it takes you too long to relay your message, then there is a good chance that it would not have as much impact.

Keep your sentences short and direct to the point. In John F. Kennedy's Presidential Inauguration speech, he inspired the nation with a speech that lasted only 14 minutes. He shared his vision of going to the moon within the decade with short statements that kept the crowd excited and expectant.

You can also keep your speech neat and clutter free by omitting unnecessary words such as "kind of," "sort of," "honestly," and "actually." Not only will it shorten your speech, but it will also diminish your credibility as these phrases often imply guesses or uncertainty.

Use relevant and up to date information. Your audience expects to learn something from listening to you. Providing them with recycled and outdated information is a waste of everybody's time. Make sure that you are able to meet their expectations by researching your topic comprehensively and providing useful information.

Add some humor to your address. Even the most serious topics or subjects can benefit from a little comic relief. While it does not need to be a long string of jokes or funny anecdotes, injecting a lighthearted comment in strategic parts of your speech can help refresh the minds of your listeners. Humor will serve as speech hooks to keep your audience interested and motivated to pay attention.

College professors who give long and at times mind exhausting lectures use this technique to keep students amused so their brains do not shut down. Adding humor does not even have to be a spoken word. One college professor who was explaining about tectonic plates to a class of freshman, decided to create light shadow figures of eagles and dogs as he was describing a fault line on a projector screen. The students were given a break from the long technical discussion for a few seconds and were able to continue listening with interest afterwards. The reason it worked was because it was unexpected and almost totally out of character.

Choose to design rather than write your speeches – Prepared speeches are written ahead of time. But when you stick to merely reading it, then it becomes public reading rather than speaking. Make sure that the speech you have prepared will allow you to be flexible when you deliver it. Keep in mind that there will be external factors such as audience reaction that you will need to consider.

Conclude with Style – The third important part of your speech is the ending. Your opening invites your audience to listen, while your closing should encourage them to take action. It should also create a pleasing conclusion to what you had invited them to take part of. While cliff hangers are great for movies and books that have a sequel, they do not work for speeches. Your message should be clearly relayed when you finish. Here are some great ways to end your speech:

Quotations that reinforce what you had discussed.

Restate your title or opening line to create a full circle.

A challenging or call to action close to encourage them to put into practice what you had talked about.

A question that you had posed at the beginning with an answer you had provided in the body. Encourage the audience to respond to create an affirmation statement.

A demonstration with a well chosen prop. You can close a book or turn off your presentation with a fitting statement.

Read Your Prepared Speech Out Loud – This will give you a chance to see the flow of your speech. It may look spectacular written on paper, but it may not have the desired effect when delivered. You can check if it has the right rhythm so it is easy to listen to. You can edit out any words or statements that may be hard to say out loud. These are stumbling blocks that you would like to avoid to make the experience more pleasant for you and your audience.

People will be hanging on to every word you deliver in your speech so ensure that you write something that will be worth listening to. If you will be talking about historical events, then it would be best to do ample research. If you will be speaking about technical process, then you will need to make sure that you provide as many details as possible.

Chapter 16: Storytelling

Telling a powerful story can be the difference between a speech that's just "okay" and a speech that's unforgettable. Furthermore, storytelling can be an excellent way to start your speech, grab your audience's attention, and introduce the theme or topic that you'll be talking to your audience about.

So then, how can you become a master storyteller and have your audience hanging on to your every word? Read on to find out...

The Secrets to Unforgettable Storytelling

Here are some different ways to ensure your story is engaging and captivating rather than boring and tedious:

- **Tailor your story to your audience.** When deciding upon a story to include in your speech, it is essential to keep your audience in mind. Storytelling can be a bit like humor: what is funny to one audience might not be funny to another. A story that you'd tell to a room of executives may be different than what would engage a room of college students, so make sure to keep your audience in mind.

- **Make sure your story has purpose.** Don't tell a story for the sake of telling a story. Your story **must** have purpose. It **must** link into the topic, theme, or objective of your speech. You must ask yourself, "What do I want my audience to get out of this story?" When it comes to storytelling, always start with the end in mind.

- **Make your story personal.** The best stories are ones that are personal. Your audience will be a whole lot more interested and engaged if it's something from your own life—an anecdote. Moreover, you can poke a little fun at yourself and expose your fears, habits, or mistakes. This lets the audience identify with you and be much more receptive to what you have to say.

- **Keep it short.** You don't want your audience to be wondering, "When the hell is this person going to finish this damn story already?!" If your story takes too long, it loses its impact. To keep it short...

- **Eliminate nonessential details.** Keep it short and snappy, sharing only the information that is necessary for the point you are making. If something doesn't add to your story, cut it out.

- **Practice makes perfect.** You will, of course, want to practice your entire speech—however you'll especially want to practice your storytelling skills so it comes out naturally and not as if you're just reading off a memorized script. You could also rehearse your story in front of a few friends and get their feedback.

- **Master your nonverbals.** Nonverbals are **especially** important when recounting an anecdote or telling a story. You can pause to build suspension, use gestures to demonstrate movement, emotion, location, shape, size, etc. You can do different voices for different characters. You can also use your voice (and body) to show excitement, sorrow, and other emotions relevant to your story.

CHAPTER 17: HOW TO WRITE YOUR FIRST PUBLIC SPEAKING PRESENTATION

A crystal-clear speech is one where the participant walks away knowing the general points you were making. You'd like your attendee's to walk away not only understanding what you stated, but the finer components of the dialogue you delivered. Supporting every single great public speaker is a fantastic presentation, and you can't afford to overlook this very important step when it comes to public speaking.

Ahead of formulating your company presentation, take a moment to make an outline. In writing on the computer, make note of the crucial specifics that you need to make. What exactly are the three most significant subjects you need your audience to walk away understanding? Often, it can be challenging to parse through your subject matter to decide these three points. Nevertheless, it truly is an essential exercise to go through. In the event you cannot identify the three principal items, then the listener will not be able to identify them either.

When you possess the three points, start to build a directory of supporting elements to each of the ideas. With respect to each subject, list out the various subtopics that you can hit on that support your key issue. Inside of these subtopics, you'll want to identify illustrations, arguments, and important particulars that you would like to offer. Make sure to type out each and every element that you need to hit upon. It is always easier to take away content later than it is to add new information.

At this stage, you will have an overview of your public speaking presentation! Congrats, because the hard work is complete! Right now is definitely the point in time for you to get started with composing your business presentation. Together with your topics, subtopics, examples, justifications, and important points, write each and every piece of the speech. Some perform best by writing it on pieces of paper and then shifting it to a presentation application. Other individuals choose to type it into software, like PowerPoint or Keynote, as they write. In either case, getting all of the content material in a demonstration format is key.

As soon as all of your content material is placed, you have got the Body of your PowerPoint presentation. Take a moment to ensure that that you're covering all of the key details, and that the subtopics flow amongst one another. The body will be the most difficult and most crucial aspect. You don't want to bombard your attendees with too much info, or bore them with too many illustrations. Perhaps its worthy of taking a part of your material out? On the other hand, too little subject matter does not build a great presentation. Good content backs up your claims, and having enough of it is crucial for the listener's to buy into your speech. In the end, striking the balance between too much and too little is continually worthy of taking into consideration.

4 DYNAMIC WAYS TO OVERCOME YOUR FEAR OF PUBLIC SPEAKING

Whether you're standing before an audience of businesspeople or your classmates, the effect is the same. All of your preparation flies out the window, your knees knock together and you must force yourself to take the stage. Public speaking is a terrifying experience for most people, but it need not be. Most people would rather have a root canal performed than speak in front of a group of people. However, performing well in this environment is, not as difficult as it sounds. In fact, it can be an enjoyable experience once you get past your fear of public speaking.

To succeed in the corporate world and to some extent your own personal world, overcoming your fear of public speaking is essential. Which poses the questions: How do you get past this seemingly insurmountable obstacle? How do you bury that fear deep in your heart and not let it overwhelm your defenses? How do you survive such a ghastly ordeal?

1. It's Not as Bad as It Seems

The very first thing you need to understand is that it is not as bad as it seems. You are focusing on the bad things, the things that might happen or could happen that would make you seem foolish or unprepared, that would make your audience laugh in derision, rather than in good humor. Such fears are natural but baseless. The audience is not there to laugh at you; they have no desire to pick apart your performance looking for absurdities. They have come to hear you speak. They believe you have valuable information to impart and they want to know what you have to say. They obviously place a great deal of value on your opinion and expertise; otherwise, they would have found somewhere else to go.

2. Everyone Experiences a Fear of Public Speaking

Everyone experiences a fear of public speaking, no matter how experienced a speaker they might be. This is important to understand - everyone feels the same fear, the same trepidation. Everyone gets the same butterflies in their stomach and experiences the same sweat-slicked palms; even those with years of experience under their belts still succumb to the fear of public speaking. So what does this tell you? It tells you two things: first, the fear you feel is natural, and nothing of which to be ashamed. Second, it tells you that you are not alone and if you work through it, you can reap tremendous rewards.

3. You are the Expert – They Picked You for a Reason

Perhaps you have the most in-depth understanding of a particular product's features. Perhaps you are responsible for developing and implementing new techniques with wide-ranging ramifications. Maybe you are the only person who understands your company's new product/service and must explain how it works to potential investors or even to company sales reps. Regardless of the reason, you are the expert - it was no mere accident you were chosen to speak at this event. You have important, vital, unique information to impart, which brings enormous value to your audience. This is your chance to share your information, so that alone should help you resolve your fear for public speaking.

4. Understand the Value You Bring to the Table

Once you understand the value you bring to the table, the rest of the process is very simple. While overcoming that fear of public speaking might seem impossible, you can use numerous techniques to help you move past it. For instance, meditation-style breathing techniques, used before you take the stage, will help slow your racing heart and stem the flood of adrenaline surging through your body.

Remember that the audience is likely not going to notice your sweating palms or your nervousness; in many ways, fear of public speaking is simply all in your mind. Having a positive mindset and the right outlook on the event will help you move past this fear. Remember, you are the expert here, take that to heart, and all else will fall into place and you can confidently deliver your engaging speech.

Chapter 18: What Is Special about This Book: An Indispensable Introduction

The Essence of Good Writing & Good Speaking

The United States National Commission on Writing has reported that businesses are spending $3.1 billion annually trying to teach employees to write clearly. Quite simply, Americans are writing nonsense at work.

Poor writing goes hand-in-hand with poor public speaking for the very good reason that they are essentially two different forms of the same thing.

Some people would argue that writing and speaking are not the same thing, that they are in fact quite different, almost to the point of being antithetical. They ground their argument on what is known as the "7 Percent Rule." This rule states that communication is only 7 percent verbal and 93 percent non-verbal, i.e. body language and vocal variety. It is the supposed result of a scientific experiment carried out at UCLA (University of California, Los Angeles) in the 1960s. However, Prof. Albert Mehrabian, who conducted the experiment, has frequently proclaimed that his research proves no such thing and has denounced the 7 Percent Rule as a gross misinterpretation of this work.

If you are inclined to believe the rule, before you go any further in this book I strongly recommend that you read Appendix A, "Debunking the 7 Percent Rule: Public Speaking's Most Pernicious Myth." Then come back and pick up your reading here. If you are already know that the rule is a myth, or have never heard of it, then just continue reading.

Much of the content of this book mirrors materials offered by Toastmasters International. TMI is a worldwide club dedicated to helping people improve their speaking and presentation skills. It has over 270,000 members in more than 100 countries. You will see a number of references to TMI throughout this book. In the spirit of full disclosure, I should mention that I was a founding member of a TMI club in Brussels, Belgium.

The March 2010 edition of the **Toastmaster**, TMI's monthly magazine, published an article titled "The Better You Write It, the Better You Say It." It makes a couple of crucial points.

Excluding pure entertainment, the objective of most speeches is to convey information, or to promote or defend a point of view. Certain tools, such as vocal variety and body language, can aid this process. But by their very nature they can communicate only emphasis or emotion.

If your words are incapable of getting your message across, then no amount of gestures or vocal variety will do it for you. Thus, when preparing a speech, your first objective must always be to carefully structure your information and look for the best words or phrases to express what

you want to say . . . But if writing your speech is the key to success, how should you go about it?"
In line with this analysis, the first purpose of this book is to lay down a few simple ground rules for writing a good speech. Once you have produced a credible, coherent speech, the second objective is to lay down a few equally simple ground rules for delivering it in the most congenial, forceful, persuasive manner.

The theoretical part of the book is divided into the following three parts.

· The Essentials of Good Writing

· The Essentials of Good Public Speaking

· The Essentials of Effective Visual Aids

These three theoretical sections are following by numerous appendices that explore certain key principles and techniques in greater detail, as well as providing some exercises to help you practice them.

Whatever your current station in life (high school student, university student, or already in the world or work), the time you have to devote reading and using this book is probably limited. It is therefore conceived so that you can pick it up and put it down at your convenience. The only requirement is that you fully read the theoretical sections **before** you go on to the examples and exercises in the appendices.

The theoretical section is quite short — about a third the total book — because the fundamental principles are few and, when explained, are almost self-evident.

It is important that you fully read the theoretical section first because each principle is closely interrelated with each other principle. They can be effectively practiced and mastered only if you already have a good idea about all of them together. Applying one principle or technique in ignorance of the others would be like driving a car without knowing how to adjust the mirror or use the turn signals. On the other hand, when applied within a clear theoretical framework, they can rapidly improve the effectiveness of your public speaking beyond anything you might have imagined.

Chapter 19: What Can You Do To Improve Your Public Speaking Skills

If you must speak in public, you'll be delighted to learn that you have various ways in which to improve your skills.

For example, you can take public speaking classes, which will help you to overcome your anxiety and nervousness, giving you the confidence to face an audience.

When you go on stage, you'll feel confident in yourself. This shows to the audience you'll be speaking to, and they'll respect you and listen to what you have to say.

People who have never spoken in public before are usually fearful – understandably! However, through formal training, you can get control over the fear and use it to your advantage when talking to the public.

Public speaking classes can be found in schools and through online training tools.

Should You Partake In A Public Speaking Class?

What is one of the first things you learn in public speaking classes? The first thing you should be taught is how to get past your anxiety.

You already know that public speaking comes with nervousness and anxiety – even experienced public speakers get nervous. It's a normal reaction, but to master the art of public speaking, it must be eliminated from the body.

If you're shy, it's imperative that you get over it, which means learning mind control techniques. Break the hold shyness has on you and you can immediately face your audience, talking to them with ease and comfort.

You take yourself into a world that nothing bothers you. Don't think so? Ask any professional public speaker how they can speak to the public, and you find that they can control their minds and nerves, giving themselves the confidence, they need.

Public speaking classes focus a good part on how to overcome anxiety and shyness. Instructors realize that anxiety can hinder you from speaking effectively, allowing you to interject emotions and feel scared to face your audience.

The only thing you can do is do your best, and when you can't break down the wall, you go back to what the classes have taught you and try again.

What else do you get from public speaking classes? They will also teach you the best ways in which to prepare your speech before the day arrives.

You'll be taught how to familiarize yourself with things around you, visualizing the venue you'll be given the speech at while practicing it.

This is the kind of things experts do to calm their nerves.

Instructors will also give you tools on how to focus. You are taught how to focus on the task at hand, ensuring no distractions enter your mind. You'll be trained to stay positive – to accept mistakes when you make speeches.

A public speaking class will help you in two ways:

Improve your public speaking skills.

Giving you tools that allow you to spontaneously speak to anyone when necessary.

These skills increase your chances for success when you need to speak in public. Your memory is going to be better, and you'll immediately think of how to get your audience's attention when you need to talk in public.

If your goal is to improve your public speaking skills, you need to be persistent in attaining your goals. If you're unable to do this, you will never overcome your fears. The more successful speeches you make, the more confident you become in yourself.

You gain a significant advantage when you take public speaking classes, training courses or workshops. By taking part in these classes, you improve your public speaking skills to use to your advantage.

What Will You Learn About Effective Public Speaking

Everybody, at some point in time, will need to speak in public – be it in class, work or funeral. It could be a person that becomes a lawyer, politician, motivational speaker, CEO, beauty queen or whatever.

Any career could entail public speaking in some form or fashion. It's important you understand what public speaking is.

A public speaker is someone who can captivate an audience almost immediately, holding it until they are done talking. The speaker can speak to the audience's heart and get their minds to think.

The speaker is impactful and quite convincing, causing the audience to change how they think and feel. Those in attendance remember what the speaker says, and feels they are a part of what the speaker is talking about.

The audience is kept entertained – nothing boring about what's being discussed. The speaker understands where the audience is coming from, making them feel at ease so the audience will trust them. The speaker understands the accountability they hold.

For you, it's important to get to this point if you want to speak successfully in public. If you don't naturally have it, you need to develop them. Remember though, a person who is naturally gifted in public speaking will still feel fear.

Effective public speaking goes beyond how you talk, what is said, the way you move and even how you stand. While these are important, they are not the heart of your public speaking.

After all, you can practice and practice, only to choke in front of your audience. You can write the best speech ever and still forget it when you're in front of an audience.

If you're going to speak effectively, you need to go beyond the physical state and go into an emotional and mental one. A speaker's mental and emotional condition will be reflected in their talk, and it's a factor that can make or break them.

What does a person need to speak publicly? Empathy, as it's how to reach their audience. It's when a person knows and cares about their audience and their reaction that the speaker can design a speech that hits their nerves.

It's important to be a people person if you want to speak effectively. This doesn't mean enjoying people or wanting to be around them. You need to have a genuine care for them.

A person who has this kind of care for people are going to speak to their emotions and make them think.

You also need to have conviction and passion about what you're talking about. You should never talk about a topic you don't have a belief in. Now true, you don't have much control over assigned topics in school, but you can still manipulate to be something that you have an interest in. When you're highly passionate about something, nothing can stop you from being an effective speaker.

The key to remember is that you can't be all about yourself and how good you speak in public. Do this, and you fail to reach out to your audience.

The key to public speaking is to affect the audience in a positive way so that you share with them a part of yourself. You want to give people some hope, encouragement and motivation.

When you reach into a person's heart, they will remember everything you told them even when the speech is over. When you touch a person so deep within themselves, they will remember who you are and what you had to say.

Something else you need to keep in mind: Never provide advice or talk about something you have no experience in or have never done.

An effective public speaker knows about her subject and will hold themselves accountable for everything they tell people.

When these characteristics are in place, everything else just falls into it.

Now, keep in mind, there are some physical factors to public speaking you need to remember:

Look in your audience's eyes, interacting with them on a personal level.

Walk around, but not so much that it distracts from your message. Never stand in one place, as your audience will become bored with the message.

When you feel nervous or jittery, take your hand and place it on the desk. This will give you some balance.

Be sure to interact with the audience and ask them questions when you're talking. If you have tangible visuals, consider passing it around so the audience can touch it for themselves. This gives them a feel for the material.

Incorporate visuals into your speech, as this livens things up for them.

Remember to practice, as that will lead to perfection.

Use every one of these principles for public speaking, so you are a more effective public speaker.

Chapter 20: What Does Breaking the Ice Actually Mean?

Summary

People speak about breaking the ice so very often without really understanding what it implies. Here is what it should mean to you.

What Does Breaking the Ice Actually Mean?

One of the terms that we use very often in our colloquial talk is "breaking the ice'.

If there is a really sexy girl in college or a handsome hunk and you manage to get a few words out of her or him for the first time, you say you have broken the ice with them. If there is someone superior to you at work and you have always been aloof and then suddenly you get them to talk with you, you say that you have broken the ice. So, does breaking the ice just mean getting on communicating terms with someone new? Or is there more to it than we generally imply?

I would say breaking the ice means getting the person interested in you. It is not just about getting them to use their vocal cords; it is about getting them interested in you at least to a little extent so that they feel it worthwhile to say something in response. When you have broken the ice with someone, they most usually speak something in response to what you are saying. This means that what you told them has held their interest.

Think about the term itself. When ice is ice, it is solid. It is stubborn and hard. But when you break it, it becomes pliable at once. It becomes fluid and starts moving. It doesn't take it long to become warm water. But as long as it is ice, it will continue to be hard. So, when you break the ice with someone, you are actually turning someone who is cold toward you into a warm, responsive person.

In other words, breaking the ice is the beginning step to any conversation.

How do you get that to happen?

All the rules I have stated in the first chapter work. You can use them, all at once, to make speaking with unfamiliar people a definite possibility. But you have to take the initiative here. Don't assume everyone to be frank and friendly and free- spirited. For most people, you will have to break the ice. This may be the route to a potential friendship or business collaboration or maybe even a relationship.

Think about it.

Break the ice more often than you do.

Chapter 21: Time Management and Goal Setting

It's a good thing to look back on what you've already achieved over the past few months or the last year but what's more productive is not looking back but moving forward. It's a better idea to look forward at the year to come especially if you are aiming to make this year the best year yet. What is it that you want to accomplish by reading this book? Certainly one of those things is improving your public speaking skills but in general in all the other areas of your life. Do you want to travel, excel in your career or achieve a fitness goal like running three half marathons over the next year? Writing this information with a date in mind on a calendar will be one way to keep this in your awareness or at least within the subconscious.

Weekly Planning

Time management can be best practised with adequate planning before your busy schedule begins. If you take time on a Friday afternoon to look at what you have ahead of yourself in the next week and then plan well for this, you're set yourself up for a more productive week ahead. It won't take too long either perhaps half an hour or so, make a brief list prioritising three important aspects of your life. Career, relationships and the relationship with yourself. Then think of a couple of things you would like to achieve in these areas of your life. This doesn't have to specifically be career, relationships and self but any three categories you deem most important in your life right now. You can mark the two-three most important things you want to be completed in a calendar or personal notebook. We all wish there were more hours in the day but if you narrow the hours of the week down you'll find there is more time available to us than we may believe. In a total week 168 hours is what we have, say you work full time then that's 50 hours right there with another 56 hours for a good 8 hours sleep every night. Even after all that time spent, you'll still have 62 hours give or take a few for everything else. If one of your goals is not relevant to your work life then here is almost three days' worth of time not at work, not sleeping, essentially free time during the evenings, and the first 90 minutes or so after you wake up. Those 62 hours can be spent wisely achieving your goals. How do you spend that time right now? Are you watching TV, movies, playing video games or scrolling through all the noise on social media? If you are serious about public speaking, then you'll easily find two hours to practise a speech that you're preparing for or alternatively you could spend this time to attend local toastmasters or some form of social club. I like to look at the concept of time this way, we all have the same hours in a day 24 but what's important is not how many hours we have but how we spend the time we do have.

What is your morning ritual?

Mornings are a powerful part of the day they determine what our moods will be like for the rest of the day, the morning sets the tone and the level of productivity we will have at work. By having a morning ritual which is positive this will automatically nudge you in the direction to have a successful more meaningful day, yet many of us don't have all too positive morning rituals, often the habitual routine is to wake up, complain about getting up first & foremost before complaining about life in general, about how tired you are and then you guessed it about going to work. This all, however, feels like a normal morning routine for most of us because we've conditioned ourselves to think this way over time. The next thing we do is make a morning coffee before turning on the news of the world to hear something bad happening in some far location. In this space of time perhaps only 10 minutes has passed and so far with this type of morning ritual its set up for stress and negativity and quite likely lower levels of productivity throughout the working hours. But if you do the opposite and wake up with a smile, think of something to appreciate go and drink a pint of water to hydrate your body and perhaps go for a morning walk or run then you'll have set yourself up for a much more successful day ahead. If you wanted to you could try and spend this precious time with your family before work this surely will help put you in a better mood and state of mind for the rest of the day ahead. If you are worried more about how limited your time is before work, then you are about waking up with a negative mindset then experiment with waking up earlier in the morning to give yourself more time. If you wake up an hour earlier than you usually do every day and you keep up with this habit for a year then you would have found a month's worth of extra time that you can spend on your goals, on your life or on improving your own public speaking skills.

Planning your weekend

While Friday is a good time to plan your week ahead, Wednesday is a good time to begin planning for the upcoming weekend. Weekends are a time off from the responsibilities at work. The weekend is often spent doing household chores and responsibilities, this isn't exactly a fulfilling break, though. That's why by planning on the prior Wednesday you can find time to spend your weekends doing the things you enjoy the most. But more importantly, it can serve to rejuvenate yourself for the week ahead. Another thing you can do is minimizing the musts, trivial activities are often enough to fill the space between any available time you may have. Examples are sending emails, laundry and grocery shopping at home, cleaning and conducting DIY tasks all day, minimising these activities is a good habit to incorporate in your life these activities don't serve your best interests, especially if this is what you're doing the most. I personally try not to check my emails more than twice a day if I can once before lunch and the other at the end of the day.

By using single blocks of time to conduct these tasks it will free up the rest of your day for the more meaningful work you want to do. If you try out these activities this will allow for a much more meaningful and productive year to come.

Much of this information is credited to Laura Vanderkam who is the author of "168 hours" and the book "I know how she does it". This author also struggled with public speaking, as a writer, she is naturally introverted which means she is most comfortable when she is in the flow writing a manuscript or blog post. She advocates that by speaking about what she loves she eventually learned to enjoy public speaking, what really helped her along the way was getting to know certain regulars who attended her speeches. To make her talks more relevant she would ask these members to keep track of their time and keep Laura up to date with the results. Laura got to know these people and they would serve as allies in the audience, helping to calm her nerves. She also recommended greeting people at the doors to serve as some form of ice breaker so the audience were not complete strangers by the time Laura went to give her presentation. This action had the effect of humanizing Laure before and putting her in an optimum state. Lastly by lifting the energy of the audience this can help to make people happier and more attentive to what you have to say, this will do wonders for most people and will allow for a far more enjoyable time on stage. This can be done by making people laugh or by getting them to stand up briefly and move about. So by applying these suggestions even those who are more introverted can achieve greatness on stage. At the very least these pointers will allow you to keep a few cards up your sleeve to use if you've encountered a low energy type audience.

Goal Setting

Goal setting is what determines whether you're growing as an individual or dying. It's been said to be the game changer in boosting performance in corporations and manifesting more positive productive behaviour among employees. A famous quote by the founder of JC Penny stores in 1902 stated "Give me a stock clerk with a goal and I'll give you a man who will make history. Give me a man with no goals and I'll give you a stock clerk". A researcher of psychology Gail Matthews observed that people who write their goals down on paper, create action plans and track their progress accordingly will achieve more goals than those who only think about their goals. Furthermore, she preaches to take these three elements to heart in any goal-setting session, these are accountability, commitment & finally writing the goals down on paper. Certain public speaking clubs like toastmasters incorporate these important elements, so why not use them with your public speaking goals? The popular acronym for goal setting is SMART, s for specific meaning be clear on what you want in life and not general, don't create a goal to earn more money make a goal with a specific digit in mind. M for Measurable, so create a simple record of your progress over time and keep up to date on this. Next is a for attainable so be realistic with what you can currently achieve although don't be too rigid with this, much of the point of goal setting is to learn new skills. What I mean is if you have a goal to run a full marathon in two weeks but you are unfit, overweight etc. Then don't be afraid to scale down and aim for something smaller like a 5k run or something of that sort. R is for relevant so looking at your deeply ingrained beliefs and principles then this is the place to find out what you really, really want. If your goals align with your ultimate purpose in life, then this is a positive sign that your goals are deeply relevant to your life purpose. If you have a compelling enough why behind your goals, then your easily conquer anyhow. The last letter of the acronym t stands for time-bound. Any goal that has no deadline is nothing more than a pipe dream. Make sure your goal has milestones so monthly or even weekly check-ins and most importantly an end date in mind. This will help to keep you on track and accountable but realize there are other things you can do to make yourself accountable. The acronym SMART will make your goals much more attainable but without any proper accountability then it's very likely you'll give up.

Accountability

There are many ways to stay accountable, keeping an accountability buddy is one way or just by being accountable to your friends and family will work to keep you going or if you're not so fond of this then you can create a consequence, tell a friend that if you don't achieve the goal then you'll have to donate a significant amount of money to a charity, make the amount significant enough that it forces you to take action towards your goal. If you end up achieving your goal in the end, then you can also do the opposite and spend your well-earned money celebrating. Remember the 3 elements of goal setting accountability, commitment and writing goals down, by doing all three this will resemble a clear benefit and advantage. Public speaking clubs are a great place to help you accomplish many of your goals, many join primarily to just improve their public speaking skills but after some time they've usually stayed for another reason. Clubs like this are great doorways to learning other essential skills like leadership, social skills and taking on more responsibility in the club. Toastmasters holds a structured education book lit for all members this book lit is called the Competent Communicator and is designed for goal setting, meaning you can adapt it to suit your needs with public speaking. If you are in a toastmaster's club already, is your goal to just finish the Competent Communicator book lit or is there a universal long-term path written out for after this? Regardless John Mclean advocates that you pull apart your specific goals into smaller bite-size tasks. By doing this the goals will not look so overwhelming and you'll see much more progress over the long run doing this.

Chapter 22: Fear is invisible

In the preceding chapter, the signs of anxiety were discussed. While simple deep breathing exercises can fix this, what if it reappeared in the middle of your speech? Again, stay confident because your audience doesn't even have the slightest clue that you're panicking!

The sweating of your hands, shaking of your knees, and your increasing pulse rate are almost impossible to be seen (at least from the audience's perspective). For a worst-case scenario, simply excuse yourself to drink a glass of water. It will not be perceived as a weakness. Anyone who has been speaking straight for an hour or more surely needs a drink. This will give you enough time to regain your composure. Remember: breathe and employ positive thoughts. It is not to kid yourself, but the self-discovery logically makes you know that there's nothing to be extremely worried about.

A social experiment done in 2003 revealed that extemporaneous speakers overrate how nervous they are. Kenneth Savitsky and Thomas Gilovich compared the results with the speakers' self-ratings versus the audience's ratings and the difference led to the conclusion.

Now that you know that experiencing fear during these instances is normal, keep your chin up and stay calm! Having a good posture not only gives you a boost of persuasiveness to the audience, it makes you confident as well! This is what a study published in the European Journal of Social Psychology had found out. When the body posture of the participants looks like in a depressed mood (i.e. sitting in a slouched manner with their heads bowed down), they exhibited inferior self-confidence. On the other hand, in those who were instructed to sit up straight with their chests out, they notably displayed greater confidence. So if you feel nervous, pose as if you're not and eventually you'll be convinced you really are confident.

The fact that you are stepping up on a stage already shows that you are special. Why your classmates voted for you, why are you being invited to talk, or why are you sent by your company for a public speaking event is because they can see something in you. So control your anxieties and prove to them you deserve the shot.

Chapter 23: Short and Long Speeches

Laura was presenting her new romance novel. Her publishing house organized a tour across the state. The first venues were a piece of cake—local coffee shops, book stores, and even parks. Every single time, some 10–25 people would gather to hear her. It was a great opportunity to be more intimate with her readers. Each talk was a success. Laura was joyfully interacting with her fans. Her fans were thankful that Laura would talk to them as if they were old friends. Furthermore, she could spend almost an hour answering questions—because, at the end, it was a conversation between Laura and her fans.

However, her publishing house wanted her to reach a wider audience. Although her fans were grateful to Laura, the publishing house needed to turn a profit from Laura's novel. Hence, they booked her to present her novel at a major book fair. Laura was really excited until the day came. The presenter introduced Laura. She walked to the stage, and then she noticed that at least 150 people were before her. There were two other writers with her, but Laura couldn't distinguish who was there to meet her.

When her turn came to speak, every single trick she used before failed. Normally, Laura would start her speech by breaking the ice with a fun and nice comment about the city or town she was visiting. When she did make the commented, nobody laughed. People were staring at her. She continued to talk, but she was becoming more nervous as time passed by. Some attendees laughed at the comments that were not supposed to be funny. More than half of the people were looking at their phones. Laura rushed her speech and tried to finish as soon as possible. In the end, from ten questions, only one was for her, and it was unrelated to her book.

What went wrong?

Well, there are crucial differences between speaking to a small group and speaking to a big group. In Laura's case, she assumed that what she used when speaking to small groups will also work for big ones. As we mentioned, Laura was able to be more intimate while speaking to small groups. An advantage of addressing a few number of people is that you can have a deeper impact on people. When Laura was addressing 10–25 people, she was able to approach almost every single person in the audience. However, this is undoable if you are delivering a speech to more than 100 people. So the first mistake was for Laura to think that she would be able to deliver a speech in the same way for small and big groups.

Think of her ice breaker. In a book fair, individuals are from very different places, and they travel to that location in order to attend the event. Laura probably didn't consider this. People didn't understand the funny comment regarding the city where the book fair happened because they could not relate to it.

Finally, it was obvious at some point that Laura was extremely nervous. The way she rushed her speech didn't improve the situation.

So what could you have done differently in the very same situation?

The obvious answer is that you should be prepared for both scenarios. Until now, we have talked about the essence of your speech, the characteristics of your audience, how to structure and prepare your speech, and how to choose the right tone, language, and supporting materials. However, we have missed how close you can be to your audience.

Small Groups

If you were to be at a party with just a few people, you can easily talk to everybody and get to know them. You can't do that in a gathering with lots of people; you won't have the time and energy to remember even the name and face of every single person. The very same applies when delivering a speech.

A great advantage of addressing a small group is that making an impact is much easier. This can benefit you when you act properly. For example, you can easily sense that something isn't going well. By being close to your audience, you'll notice if people aren't relating to what you're saying. You can then change course rapidly and get back on track by making your speech more interesting. You can subsequently go deeper into some parts of your speech. The key is to pay close attention to how people are reacting to your speech and react properly (Wilder, 1999).

However, be aware that speaking to small groups come with different dynamics. More precisely, interacting with small groups can smoothly become conversations between you and the audience. In big groups, questions are often asked at the end. Small groups, on the other hand, may require you to stop in the middle of your speech to answer questions. Stay chill and take advantage of the situation. There's a reason why sales pitches are normally performed in small groups. This is because the seller wants everything that is said to be crystal clear. Engagement is crucial in achieving this. Allow (or even encourage) people ask you questions in the middle of your speech. You can then explain further anything that is unclear. What is more, you can go deeper into something that your audience finds interesting.

Lastly, you can further interact with your audience by asking them to make something related to your topic. Let's say that you're talking about social media. You can ask people to check their phones and talk about the latest trending posts in their feeds. Or even start a conversation about the issues they like or dislike the most about being on social media. This can be quite exciting and interesting for people because it isn't just about you explaining a given topic. You show that you wish to know them better. And naturally, it gives you a shot to further explain the topic. It's really a matter of you being creative and capable of connecting with people by engagement.

Large Groups

Speaking before large groups is a completely different experience. Large crowds could be intimidating for first-timers. The first thing to remember is that the techniques of public speaking for small groups rarely work in this case. Being in front of many individuals can create a barrier.

For this type of scenario, it is convenient to have a much more generic approach. While in a small group you are more certain about the features of your audience, in a large group, you are addressing a very mixed group of people. Likewise, it's harder to know how acquainted you are with your topic. Although you should still try to do so, don't worry if you can't figure out entirely the profile of your audience.

The interaction with the audience will naturally be much less fluid. However, you still need to try to read all the signs that they might be throwing at you. Wait to see if the audience laughs at something that was supposed to be funny or if you hear any murmuring after your shared a shocking fact. In these circumstances, however, it's quite likely that questions will come last. In this sense, keep in mind that questions might be tougher than with a smaller group. This is because the audience tends to fall shy to make hard questions around a small number of people, but they could be more assertive with larger ones. However, in larger groups, you don't need to interact further with a person asking problematic questions since there might be more questions to answer.

Recap

You've guessed it. It's time to go back to our book-long exercise. We'll play with your speech a little bit now.

First, I want you to retailor your speech as if you were to present it to a group of 10 people. In this sense, try to make it much more interactive. Think of how you can interact with your audience and engage with participants. Plan some dynamic way so that your speech isn't just a monologue but a dialogue.

Second, make a second version of your speech. This time, assume that you were to speak before 100 people. Since this will be less interactive, think of ways to attract the attention of your audience. Try to make this version more generic compared to the first one. Imagine, as well, what type of questions attendees might ask you.

We'll check this exercise one last time in the conclusion.

CHAPTER 24: Delivering Your Speech

A great speech on paper is not a great speech unless it is delivered effectively. The number one thing that you can do to improve your delivery is to practice. Know your content. Know your transitions. Know your timing. Stand up and deliver your speech in the bathroom before you deliver it in the boardroom. Here are a few things to keep in mind for an effective delivery:

Grab Attention at the Beginning, and Close with a Dynamic End.

Do you enjoy hearing a speech start with "Today I'm going to talk to you about X"? Most people don't. Instead, use a startling statistic, an interesting anecdote, or a concise quotation. Conclude your speech with a summary and a strong statement that your audience is sure to remember.

Walk on Stage with passion

As a professional speaker, you have to always walk on stage with passion and let it look as if you belong there.

And that means everywhere you go because the world is your stage. This doesn't mean that you ever appear arrogant or controlling – you simply give the impression that you are comfortable and belong there. Show them you are comfortable in the role. Comfort goes hand-in-hand with confidence and leadership. Even in an unfamiliar situation, make other people feel your confidence and you will come across like a leader.

Display a confident attitude

After you have chosen a topic in which you are interested, finished your research, analyzed your audience, organized your ideas, and practiced your speech, you're dressed for the occasion, and you arrived early at the location of your speech, you are passionate about your topic, and you are happy to have the opportunity to tell your audience about it. So when it is your turn to get up and speak, put into motion the positive scenario you previously visualized:

Face your audience and look at all your listeners.

Take a deep breath and smile.

Clearly, confidently, and enthusiastically begin your speech.

Watch for Feedback and Adapt to It.

Keep the focus on the audience. Gauge their reactions, adjust your message, and stay flexible. Delivering a canned speech will guarantee that you lose the attention of or confuse even the most devoted listeners.

Eye Contact

Eye contact is a speaker's ability to have visual contact with everyone in the audience. Your audience should feel that you are speaking to them, not simply uttering main and supporting points. If you are new to public speaking, you may find it intimidating to look at the audience in the eye, but if you think about speakers you have seen who did not maintain eye contact, you will realize why this aspect of speech delivery is important. Without eye contact, the audience begins to feel invisible and unimportant, as if the speaker is just speaking to hear his/her own voice. Eye contact lets your audience feel that your attention is on them, not solely on the cards in front of you.

Posture

"Stand up tall!" When you stand up straight, you communicate to your audience, without saying a word, that you hold a position of power and take your position seriously. If, however, you are slouching, hunched over, or leaning on something, you could be perceived as ill-prepared, anxious, lacking in credibility, or not serious about your responsibilities as a speaker. While speakers often assume a more casual posture as a presentation continues (especially if it is a long one, such as a ninety-minute class lecture), it is always wise to start by standing up straight and putting your best foot forward. Remember, you only get one shot at making a first impression, and your body's orientation is one of the first pieces of information audiences use to make that impression.

Facial Expressions

Faces convey so much information. As speakers, we must be acutely aware of what our face looks like while speaking. While many of us do not look forward to seeing ourselves on videotape, often the only way you can critically evaluate what your face is doing while you are speaking is to watch a recording of your speech. If the video is not available, you can practice speaking in front of a mirror.

There are two extremes you want to avoid: no facial expression and over-animated facial expressions. First, you do not want to have a completely blank face while speaking. Some people just do not show much emotion with their faces naturally, but this blankness is often increased when the speaker is nervous. Audiences will react negatively to the message of such a speaker because they will sense that something is amiss. If a speaker is talking about the joys of Disney World and his face doesn't show any excitement, the audience is going to be turned off to the speaker and his message. On the other extreme end is the speaker whose face looks like that of an exaggerated cartoon character. Instead, your goal is to show a variety of appropriate facial expressions while speaking.

Body Movement

Unless you are stuck behind a podium because of the need to use a fixed microphone, you should never stand in one place during a speech. However, movement during a speech should also not resemble pacing. As speakers, we must be mindful of how we go about moving while speaking. One common method for easily integrating some movement into your speech is to take a few steps any time you transition from one idea to the next. By only moving at transition points, not only do you help focus your audience's attention on the transition from one idea to the next, but you also are able to increase your nonverbal immediacy by getting closer to different segments of your audience.

Body movement also includes gestures. These should be neither overdramatic nor subdued. At one extreme, arm-waving and fist-pounding will distract you from your message and reduce your credibility. At the other extreme, refraining from the use of gestures is the waste of an opportunity to suggest emphasis, enthusiasm, or other personal connection with your topic.

There are many ways to use gestures. The most obvious are hand gestures, which should be used in moderation at carefully selected times in the speech. If you overuse gestures, they lose meaning. However, the well-placed use of simple, natural gestures to indicate emphasis, direction and size are usually effective.

Normally, a gesture with one hand is enough. Rather than trying to have a gesture for every sentence, use just a few well-planned gestures. It is often more effective to make a gesture and hold it for a few moments than to begin waving your hands and arms around in a series of gestures.

Volume

Volume refers to how loud or soft your voice is. As with speaking rate, you want to avoid the extremes of being too loud or too soft, but still vary your volume within an acceptable middle range. When speaking in a typically sized classroom or office setting that seats about twenty-five people, using a volume a few steps above a typical conversational volume is usually sufficient. When speaking in larger rooms, you will need to project your voice. You may want to look for nonverbal cues from people in the back rows or corners, like leaning forward or straining to hear, to see if you need to adjust your volume more. Obviously, in some settings, a microphone will be necessary to be heard by the entire audience. Like rate, audiences use volume to make a variety of judgments about a speaker. Softer speakers are sometimes judged as meek, which may lead to lowered expectations for the speech or less perceived credibility. Loudspeakers may be seen as overbearing or annoying, which can lead audience members to disengage from the speaker and message. Be aware of the volume of your voice and, when in doubt, increase your volume a notch, since beginning speakers are more likely to have an issue of speaking too softly rather than too loudly.

Articulation refers to the clarity of sounds and words we produce. If someone is articulate, they speak words clearly, and speakers should strive to speak clearly. Poor articulation results when speakers do not speak clearly. For example, a person may say "dint" instead of didn't, "gonna" instead of going to, "wanna" instead of wanting to, or "hunnerd" instead of hundred.

Unawareness and laziness are two common challenges to articulation. As with other aspects of our voice, many people are unaware that they regularly have errors in articulation. Recording yourself speak and then becoming a higher self-monitor are effective ways to improve your articulation.

Personal Appearance

Looking like a credible and prepared public speaker will make you feel more like one and will make your audience more likely to perceive you as such. This applies to all speaking contexts: academic, professional, and personal. Although the standards for appropriate personal appearance vary between contexts, meeting them is key. You may have experienced a time when your vocal and physical delivery suffered because you were not "dressed for the part.". Ideally, you should be comfortable in the clothes you're wearing. If the clothes are dressy, professional, and nice but ill-fitting, then the effect isn't the same. Avoid clothes that are too tight or too loose. Looking the part is just as important as dressing the part, so make sure you are cleaned and groomed in a way that's appropriate for the occasion.

Take Your Time

Take your time and allow everyone to absorb what you are saying. A speech is not a race. Start slow and if you see that your audience wants you to speak a little faster, then, and only then, start to pick up the pace.

Have a Backup Plan

If you have supplementary materials such as visual aids or a PowerPoint presentation, have a backup plan in place in case some piece of equipment doesn't work. You may want to have printouts just in case a computer or projector doesn't work.

Similarly, if you've memorized your speech or maybe reading from a teleprompter, have a printed copy of your speech or an outline of your speech on hand just in case you get a case of stage fright or equipment fails.

Conclusion

Only bad speakers are alike." Good speakers are distinguished by individual uniqueness. They are unique by their inherent manner of constructing a speech, selecting language means, influencing the audience in the process of speech. Making an individual style is an important speaker task.

If we want to fully master the art of public speaking, we start two tasks today. The first is a plan and analysis of self-development as a speaker. The second is the "Memorial" (your name). We bring into it all the interesting speech turns that we hear in the speech of other people, on TV and radio, meetings in books. Still - vivid quotes, juicy jokes, etc. This is our lexical piggy bank. Every time we want to add juiciness to our text, look there and be sure to find something suitable.

The book has presented you with a detailed technology for preparing public speaking. Among the tasks to be solved is developing the skill of effective public behavior, developing the potential of the individual, improving life through polishing the gift of eloquence. The proposed exercises were to help you see your abilities in the field of public expression, develop them, and put them into service to achieve personal and social tasks.

I wish you all the best in your endeavor!

www.ingramcontent.com/pod-product-compliance
Lightning Source LLC
Chambersburg PA
CBHW071844080526
44589CB00012B/1105